I Will Take Care of You
FOR THE REST OF YOUR LIFE

I Will Take Care of You
FOR THE REST OF YOUR LIFE

RUTH MARTINEZ

CITATION

ESV
Unless otherwise indicated, all scripture quotations are from
The Holy Bible, English Standard Version® (ESV®). Copyright ©2001
by Crossway Bibles, a division of Good News Publishers.
Used by permission. All rights reserved.

KJV
Scripture quotations marked KJV are from the Holy Bible,
King James Version (Authorized Version). First published in 1611.
Quoted from the KJV Classic Reference Bible, Copyright © 1983
by The Zondervan Corporation.

Print information available on the last page.

Rev. date: 10/22/2021

To order additional copies of this book, contact:
Xlibris
844-714-8691
www.Xlibris.com
Orders@Xlibris.com
553389

Contents

In Memory of Josephine Rios

Mom's Life

My mother, Josephine Florinda Real, born April 30, 1914, was a daughter, sister, mother, grandmother, great grandmother, aunt and friend. She was born in Mulege and had three brothers, Angel, Abraham and Manuel. Her parents, especially her mother, were devout Catholics who later converted to Christianity. Josephine's mother was strict and legalistic. She sheltered her daughter from the "real world."

At age 8, Josephine's family traveled by boat to California. They lived in El Cajon on a lot with three houses. Here, she lived a good part of her life. Directly behind the property was a small church, La Primera Iglesia Bautista, where she attended and raised her children and grandchildren. At this church, she played the piano, taught Sunday school and Vacation Bible School. Years later, another denomination purchased the church and Josephine continued worshipping at the First Baptist Church, where she became a member of the choir and sang in the annual Christmas Contatas.

Mom attended school up to the 6th grade. She had to discontinue her education in order to assist her parents by working in the cotton fields. Years later, she attended Adult School to learn English fluently.

With little resources, Josephine learned how to read, write English and play the piano.

At age 14, she fell extremely ill with tuberculosis and as she put it, wanted to die. When Mom looked into the mirror, all she could see were skin and bones. The Lord healed Mom for He had a greater plan for her life. She loved her parents and was very close to them. Certainly, being the only girl in the family, she may have been somewhat spoiled.

Years later as a young woman, Mom fell deeply in love with a man who owned Salazar's Market, a neighborhood store down the street from her home. Although he was also in love with her, he was devoted to his mother and their family business. Mom was so heartbroken and angry that she was determined to marry the next man she met.

At the time, Mom was working in downtown San Diego at the Del Coronado Hotel where she would take the bus in front of the Horton Plaza. Here, she met a sailor, and within months, the two married. Mom was in her late 20s, beautiful with an outgoing personality. She was at times flirtatious even during her later years. Mom was friendly and enjoyed interacting with people.

During the early part of their marriage, they lived in San Jose. Shortly, they had their first son, Samuel David and three years later, she had her first daughter, Sylvia Linda. Years passed when she discovered her husband was having an extramarital affair with a former girlfriend. Mom was a devout Christian who was extremely troubled by this. Shortly after her husband went to war and with the assistance of her Pastor providing Biblical counsel, they separated and divorced. Mom returned to El Cajon to reunite with her family.

My maternal grandfather practiced infidelity towards my grandmother. Due to his lifestyle, she contracted syphilis and became terribly ill. At that time, medicine was not as advanced so her symptoms worsened and she eventually became paralyzed. Josephine was by her mother's side, providing care around the clock until she passed away in 1948. At that point, Mom manifested her generosity by offering care to her father who remarried and later passed on.

Mom was an exemplary daughter who tended to both parents. For many years, she remained single and raised two children, in the Lord, including her nephew, Steven. Meanwhile, she was extremely active in the church, teaching and playing the piano. She experienced some difficult and lonely times in her life, but she remained strong in the Lord and faithfully served Him. She was healthy, active and attractive. It was in her small church where she met Jose Rios, who pursued her relentlessly. After gaining the approval of her parents, she finally married him. He regularly attended church with his big Bible in hand. He was a man on a mission. She was 39-years-old and he was in his early 20s. They were years apart in age. Yes, Mom robbed the cradle but looking at their wedding picture, you would never know it because she looked amazing! Shortly after, she had her second son, Jose Rodolfo. Within a few months, due to her husband's job, they moved to Escondido. A year later, she had her second daughter, Ruth Ann. The following year the family returned to El Cajon, where her husband, Jose, had purchased a house on Willet Street. He worked in construction, eventually owned his business along with his brother-in-law, and made a great living.

We lived in a predominately white neighborhood. At the time there were few Mexicans who lived in El Cajon. Actually, we were the few. It was in this house where the family gathered to celebrate Christmas, sing carols, as Mom played the piano, eat menudo, tamales, and wait until midnight to open gifts. Mom's favorite carol was, "Oh Holy Night." There were many wonderful memories and happy times. Mom loved family gatherings. She lived in this house for years, until all her children grew and either married or like Ruth, went away to attend college.

Mom was married to Jose for over 20 years. Once again, she faced another love triangle, as her husband also had an affair. He married this woman but the marriage only lasted six months and was quickly annulled. My parents were separated but still living in the same house. Dad decided he would not leave our home until all of us were living independently. I never understood why. Shortly after I married, they divorced and Mom remained single for the rest of her life.

She always enjoyed her friends and ministered to the young women in her church, taking them out to eat, giving them rides to church and even allowing them to live in her home, when necessary. She practiced her gifts of generosity and hospitality.

Mom settled down in El Cajon and said she would never leave unless her apartment burned down. Years later, her neighbor, a man with mental issues, went on a shooting rage, killing women and children. Looking out from her bedroom window, Mom witnessed a woman, lying in the parking lot, bleeding to death. But she remained quiet, in her apartment, until the police safely walked her outside. She was very courageous. This man had been her neighbor for years. The Lord protected her.

After this tragedy, Mom relocated to Escondido, she attended the church me and my children were attending at the time, Bethel Baptist. Again, she joined the choir and met some beautiful friends, sisters in the Lord, who a few years later went to be with Him. She also became the pianist for a Spanish Mission where she met her hermanos y hermanas en Cristo.

In 2001, her eldest son joined Set Free, which was a rehabilitation and a spiritual repentance for him. Prior to this, he lived a lifestyle of alcohol and drugs, which eventually put him into a coma. The doctors told us he wasn't going to make it. Mom and I flew to the State of Washington to be by his side to pray. As soon as we arrived at the hospital, I began looking up churches in the phone book, asking brothers and sisters in the Lord, to come and pray for him. Meanwhile, Mom and I stayed with him for four days, praying and singing praises in his hospital room. Those passing, in the hallway, heard us while some recognized the songs. We whispered prayers into his ear, knowing he could hear. The churches responded and gathered to pray. God was near and present amongst His children. As we all gathered around Sam's bed, the doctor came into the room to tell us he probably would not make it. Mom looked him straight in the eyes and said, "You can say what you want, but God has the final word." Hallelujah! I loved that about Mom! Not only did she have the faith but she also had the courage to proclaim it! The doctor calmly agreed. After four days, we had to leave, but we trusted the Lord for healing. As we flew away, I said, "Lord, we put him in your hands." The next day we received a call from his son telling us that he had awakened from his coma and was walking, talking and eating. Thank you, Jesus! The Lord is faithful to His Word. Jesus said, "And whatever you ask in My name, that I will do, that the Father may be glorified in the Son" (John 14: 13). His Word is powerful! "For the word of God is living and powerful, and sharper than any two-edged sword, piercing even to the division of soul and spirit, and of joints and marrow, and is a discerner of the thoughts and intents of the heart" (Hebrews 4:12).

My brother Sam eventually relocated to Escondido but still needed help. I introduced him to Set Free Ministry where, finally, he was set free but only for a season. We joined the church to support his decision to follow the Lord. My daughter and I served in the children's ministry and I also taught the Woman's Bible Study, which

Mom participated and enjoyed. It was refreshing and new as we witnessed my brother serving the Lord, playing the congas in the praise and worship band. It was our season, as me and my brother enjoyed going to church and Christian concerts together. We finally had Christ in common. Sadly, after two years at Set Free, he fell back into his drinking patterns and as a result, passed away in 2003. Once again, it was Mom's faith which sustained her through this difficult time. She didn't understand why the Lord had taken him but she knew Sam had abused his body, for too long. The Lord knew how he would continue to live his life and because God is gracious and loving, He took Sam home. "For the wages of sin is death, but the free gift of God is eternal life in Christ Jesus our Lord" (Romans 6:23). The last church Mom attended was mine, the Rock Church, in San Diego. She referred to Pastor Miles as, "The Funny Pastor."

Due to her upbringing, Mom had little tact but she always meant well. She was, blatantly, honest which many times was perceived as insensitive. But her intentions were never to offend, for if she had known she would have, quickly, asked for forgiveness. After living with us a short while, Mom moved into a senior citizen complex. The only thing she didn't like about this place was that the residents were too old. Mom was in her 80s, but she still had this youthfulness about her. She preferred the company of younger women. She remained strong and healthy but her memory was faltering. It was apparent she needed to return to live with us again. I prayed and asked the Lord for guidance. He told me to begin looking for a 4-bedroom house which would accommodate both Mom and my children. Although she liked her independence, she didn't enjoy living alone.

In 2000, we began to look for a home. One Sunday afternoon, as my daughter Lea and I were leaving church, we spotted an Open House sign. We turned into the neighborhood, saw the house, walked inside, and immediately knew this was the place for us. The Lord made a way and provided this house for our family and others who would share in the blessing.

We loved and cherished her presence. Mom made it a home, filling it with laughter, playing the piano and sweetly singing her favorite Baptist hymns. Mom's great sense of humor and funny mannerisms brought joy to our hearts. This would become the last season in our journey, sharing our lives together.

Mom left her legacy, one in which will carry on for generations. "For the Lord is good; His mercy is everlasting, And His truth endures to all generations" (Psalm 100:5). To this day, the Lord continues to answer the prayers of her family as we recall her words of wisdom and Godly counsel, which continues to resonate with us. But most of all, we treasure her exemplary life which speaks louder than words. She lived a long life and was faithful to her God, the Lord Jesus Christ. Leaving 1 son, 2 daughters, 8 grandsons, 1 granddaughter, 14 great grandchildren and both nieces and nephews. She outlived both of her ex-husbands who were younger, all of her siblings, two nephews, eldest son and all of her closest friends. A joyful reunion in heaven has taken place but greater joy is to come!

> Jesus said, "As the Father loved me, I also have loved you; abide in my love."
> "These things I have spoken to you, that my joy may remain in you, and that your joy may be full!" (John 15: 9, 11).

Every birthday, Mom would say, "I don't know if I'll be here another year." My thought was that she would remain till the end. I attribute her long life to our Heavenly Father, who also taught her how to live a healthy life. Mom took good care of herself. I always admired the way she groomed herself and even exercised. I still remember how everyday she would lie down to rest. It was during those times she would read the Bible along with her health magazines. She was intrigued as she educated herself. Not only did she share her knowledge but she began to put it, into practice. Back in the day, she was already reading the ingredients on food labels and warning me of the junk that was in our food. Mom was ahead of her time. I remember how she would wipe the excess salt off her chips because she learned too much salt was not good. Although her weakness was sweets, apple pie, she became more disciplined as she grew older. Mom was not one to join a gym neither do excessive exercise but she loved to go on brisk walks. She would tell me how it was good exercise. So, gladly, I would accompany her and we would enjoy our walks together. Mom was also, extremely, meticulous. Our house was always clean! I mean sparkling clean! She taught my siblings and me how to clean the house, beginning with our bedrooms. By the time I left home, I was cleaning the entire house! With all that practice, I became an expert. It's no wonder my home reflects, Mom's example of both Godliness and cleanliness. She taught me so much by her example. I appreciated her zeal for life and persistence in pleasing her God.

Mom's favorite chapter in the Bible was Psalm 91. Here are a few verses taken from that chapter.

> "He who dwells in the secret place of the Most High
> Shall abide under the shadow of the Almighty. I will say to the Lord,
> "He is my refuge and my fortress, My God, in Him I will trust."
> He shall cover you with His feathers,

And under His wings you shall take refuge;

Because you have made the Lord, who is my refuge, even

the Most High, your dwelling place,

No evil shall befall you,

Nor shall any plague come near your dwelling;

He shall call upon Me, and I will answer him;

With long life I will satisfy him, And show him my

salvation."

These were some of Mom's favorite sayings, which she used, frequently.

"Are you a Christian?"

"Do you go to church?"

"Read your Bible."

"Did you wash your hands?"

"Don't touch my hair."

"Golly, man."

"I love you too, honey."

MY STORY

I was born in Escondido, California, in 1955 at Palomar Hospital. A year later, we relocated to El Cajon, where I completed my studies and graduated from high school. I was the youngest of four children, two brothers and one sister. Our mother was born in Baja, a born again Christian and our father was from Mexico, a hardworking man and great provider, but he was an alcoholic. Needless to say, I grew up in a dysfunctional family.

By age three, Mom noticed my sensitivity towards the Spirit of God. I was extremely young when she shared the gospel with me. I learned Jesus loved me and died on the cross and shed His blood for my sins. "For God so loved the world that He gave His only begotten Son, that whoever believes in Him should not perish but have everlasting life. For God did not send His Son into the world to condemn the world, but that the world through Him might be saved" (John 3:16, 17). I took this matter quite personal and cried uncontrollably. I was deeply touched by such insight that I prayed asking Jesus to come into my heart. At that moment, I fell deeply in love with Jesus Christ. He captivated my heart and became the love of my life. It was the beginning of a God-predestined journey of our lives together. In retrospect, I clearly see how the Lord created a perfect path for me and my Mother to experience a unique and beautiful relationship. Mom was my example, teacher, mentor, and best friend. "Train up a child in the way he should go. And when he is old, he will not depart from it." (Proverbs 22: 6).

I had a fairly happy childhood, although I had seen and heard things I should not have. I feared my Dad and observed my siblings and cousins, closely. I grew up in an environment where alcohol, drugs, and all other things that go along with that lifestyle, were common. Honestly, I felt as if I did not belong in my family. I didn't think of myself as superior. I just knew I was different and didn't fit in. I grew up with a majority of men in my family who were worldly, but respected me. Sometimes, I overheard their derogatory comments about women. We often traveled to Mexico, and as a little girl, I remember how the men made such comments. Needless to say, it gave me a negative impression of them, altogether. Later on, as I began to develop physically, I was unhappy by the way men looked at me. I didn't welcome that kind of attention. A big part of it, began with my Dad, who loved women.

Growing up with parents of extreme lifestyles was hardly exemplary. But sometimes you were caught between the two extremes. Of course, our nature as humans is to satisfy the fleshly desires. But, as a born-again child of God, He gave me a discerning spirit. I knew much of what I had witnessed was wrong. Sadly, I have family members who are still struggling with addictions and others who have suffered devastating consequences.

For the most part, I was an obedient child because of my love for Jesus, Mom, and fear of my Dad. In some ways, I thought my parents were stricter and expected more from me. For example, one day I was late coming home from school when Mom told Dad to spank me. He had never spanked me because when Dad was a child, his parents were abusive, often whipping him. He pretended to spank me only to appease her. Neither did Mom ever lay a hand on me. However, I witnessed how she took the belt to my siblings, when they began testing the waters. Mom was strict with us and legalistic. Besides the common ones, she taught us that playing cards, going to movies, and dancing were sinful. As I grew older, she became less legalistic and a bit more lenient. Neither was Mom affectionate. Many times when I'd hug her she would not return the affection. Her arms would remain hanging by her sides. I thought it was odd, especially, coming from Mom who was so in love with Jesus. I asked her why she didn't wrap her arms around me. Her response was that her parents did the same with her. She went on to say that they never even told her that they loved her. But she knew by the way they treated her. I literally took Mom's arms and placed them around me, teaching her how to respond to my love. She also had to practice saying the words, "I love you." But in her later years she, naturally, said those words, often, to express the depths of her love. Towards the end of her life, she repeatedly, spoke these words, "I love you, too, Honey."

When I was thirteen, my Dad told me how he didn't want me to grow up to be like him. The very first time I talked back, telling him respectfully that I would not grow up to be like him, he slapped me across the face. At the age of sixteen, when I fell ill with the flu, he asked me if I was pregnant. Wow! I was shocked and deeply hurt by this accusation. The fact that he would think this of me was quite disturbing. However, it proved that he did not know me. Sadly, I didn't have a close relationship with my Dad for a great part of my life. It took a while for me to even call him, "Dad." For most of my childhood I called him, "Cuco." Although it seemed awkward to me, it was what he wanted. Since I did not have a Godly father, I looked to the Reverend Billy Graham and my Pastors as my spiritual fathers, including those on the radio.

Mom would always gather us around the TV to watch the Reverent Billy Graham. I grew up listening to his powerful sermons, and singing along with the choir, "Just as I Am." One of my dreams was to see him in person. I joined a team of counselors for his last crusade, in San Diego. My choice was to pray with women and children. I, distinctly, remember that night. It was amazing to be in the midst of this tremendous gathering of people who came to hear the word of God from His servant. After preaching the sermon, Billy Graham gave the invitation as the choir began to sing. As a child, I'd always cry during this part of the service because it reminded me of my own conversion. I walked onto the field and got as close as I could to the stage to see him. Then I stopped, bowed my head, and began to pray. When I looked up there was a girl with her father, standing right in front of me. She was 9 years old. My age, when the Lord healed me! I've always had a special place in my heart for 9 year olds. It's no wonder the Lord allowed me to teach fourth graders most of my career. I prayed with her to receive Jesus! In fact, all the children I prayed with, that weekend, were 9 year olds! It so happened that this girl went to a church right across the street from where I lived. I went to visit and witnessed her singing in the praise and worship team. It was very special. Before I walked away from the stage that night, in awe, I thanked the Lord for making my dream come true!

I always prayed for Dad's salvation. At one time, I attended a Pentecostal Church that would pray in tongues and dance in the Spirit for hours. Mom allowed me go on Sunday nights. I prayed for Dad and my family, for long periods of time, until Mom literally pulled me away from the altar because of school the following day. After all the years of praying for Dad, little did I know that I would be instrumental in praying the prayer of salvation with him, in my home, as we watched the Reverend Billy Graham. It was an answered prayer, which I had waited for so long.

The Bible says, "Pray without ceasing" (1 Thessalonians 5: 17). In other words, keep praying. PUSH! (Pray Until Something Happens) Another passage reads, "And the prayer of faith shall save the sick, and the Lord shall raise him up; and if he have committed sins, they shall be forgiven him. Confess your faults one to another and pray one for another, that you may be healed. The effectual fervent prayer of a righteous man avails much" (James 5:15, 16).

I'm thankful that after much counseling, due to my divorce, I was able to reconcile my relationship with my Dad, telling him I loved and forgave him. After his conversion, we were able to share some great times! We went to church together! Watching Dad worship the Lord was unbelievable! One special day, Mom and Dad came with me to prepare my classroom for the new school year. Mom came often, for she enjoyed it. But this time Dad came along. For the very first time in my life, I felt like we were a family reunited in Christ! Watching my elderly parents sharing together in this endeavor which we all had a part in accomplishing, was heavenly.

In spite of my surroundings, I chose not to drink alcohol, especially after Dad insisted that I take a sip of his beer. I still remember the nasty taste! I chose not to take drugs, although the smell of weed became common. I chose not to take pills, even though a variety of multicolored ones, filled a large jar on top of the toilet, which Mom and I would dust frequently when cleaning the bathroom. I chose, by the grace of God, to obey my parents, even when Dad would often tell me to get him a glass of beer from his cag in the garage. I obeyed him and did it so often that I became an expert at putting a head on the beer. It gave me a sense of pride, knowing that it pleased him. Finally, Mom put a stop to it, telling him that I was not his bar tender.

After my first divorce while I was in my early thirties, I made choices; some out of pure ignorance and others knowingly. An example was going to nightclubs with my sister, who was more the quiet type but after a few drinks, she became a different person and I liked that side of her. I was too naïve to understand what was taking place, but I enjoyed dancing while sipping on virgin Piña Coladas. When I realized what was happening, in this worldly atmosphere, I immediately stopped going.

"Prove all things; hold fast that which is good, abstain from all appearance of evil" (1 Thessalonians 5: 21, 22).

Regardless of my foolishness, the Lord protected me from a poisonous lifestyle and for that reason, I am forever grateful that He kept His hand of protection over me.

One thing I do regret was Mom putting me on a pedestal and raising me as if I was this perfect child. It seemed like others could indulge in sinful acts, but if I did, I was looked upon with greater condemnation. It was unfair and set an unrealistic standard for me, one which I could not uphold. At one point in my Christian walk, I contemplated thoughts of self- righteousness. I never thought I was better neither did I think less of others, but due to my upbringing, I thought that I would never do the things that many others were practicing. How ignorant! The Lord reminded me of my sinful nature. The Bible says, "For all have sinned and fall short of the glory of God" (Romans 3:23).

This means no one is exempt. ALL, have sinned. Many believe they are good people and will ascend to heaven. However, this is incorrect. It is a lie from Satan. Good attributes come from God.

They're not acknowledged because those who are lost, walking in darkness, do not recognize Him.

The Bible says, "So God created man in His own image, in the image of God created he him; male and female created he them" (Genesis 1:27).

"As it is written, There is none righteous, no, not one" (Romans 3:10). "The fool has said in his heart, there is no God" (Psalm 141:1).

"Every way of a man is right in his own eyes, but the Lord weighs the hearts" (Proverbs 21:2).

"There is a way that seems right to a man, but its end is the way of darkness" (Proverbs 16:25).

The good qualities and deeds that many want to own, come from our Creator. All of us have sinned against God and for that reason, Christ died to save us from our sins. As long as we are in this fleshly body, we will have tendencies to succumb to our fleshly desires. However, I have found that as I surrender my will to His, and grow in Him, I will not repeat previous acts of sins. I pray continually to not offend my God, by giving into my selfish will. I refuse to say, "I'm not perfect," because many Christians use that excuse as a cop out, somehow, giving themselves permission to sin.

"What shall we say then? Shall we continue in sin, that grace may abound? Certainly, not! How shall we who died to sin live any longer in it?" (Romans 6:1, 2)

We have the freedom to choose, as children of Almighty God. We are not victims of our flesh. "If we confess our sins, He is faithful and just to forgive us our sins and to cleanse us from all unrighteousness" (1 John 1:9).

"Therefore, if anyone be in Christ, he is new creation; old things have passed away; behold all things have become new" (2 Corinthians 5:17).

Mom was my source of strength and encouragement. She was the one who kept me focused on Jesus. As a child, I practiced the gifts He had given me by sharing stories about Jesus to my friends. One of the boys in my neighborhood was born with a heart condition. The Lord impressed upon my heart to share the gospel with him. He accepted Jesus and months later he passed away. Hallelujah! He's in Heaven! This was the beginning of my long journey using these gifts for His glory.

My school years were exciting. I enjoyed school but I was not the brightest student. I was insecure and desired to be accepted by my peers. I will always remember in my third grade class, how I had asked my teacher, Mrs. Caldwell, if I could sing a song during "sharing time." From that point on, she often announced to the class that I was going to sing. I sang about Jesus. I shared the gospel without realizing it. It was such a thrill! In fourth grade, our family had taken a trip to Mexico, where I contracted Hepatitis A. I became extremely, ill. The doctor recommended hospitalization, however, Mom insisted on taking care of me. For months, I was unable to attend school and remained secluded in my bedroom, highly contagious. Since Mom was vaccinated, she was the only one who could enter my bedroom to feed me and give me my medicine. I longed to go outside. Together, we prayed and within four months the Lord healed me! Thank you, Jesus! This was the first miracle I had ever experienced!

The following Sunday, Mama Lee, our missionary friend, asked me to stand and give thanks to the Lord for what He had done for me. "In everything give thanks; for this is the will of God in Christ Jesus concerning you" (1Thessalonians 5:18).

For the first time, I shared my testimony. I thought my cousins would laugh at me because that is what we did, at times. But that day, I stood up and thanked the Lord for healing me. Embarrassed, I quickly sat down and buried my face into my hands. The room was silent. No one laughed.

I always loved going to church with Mom. We often sang duets together. One of our favorite hymns was, "Great is Thy Faithfulness." I admired her talent, as she played the piano. As a child, I sat next to her while she played at home, wishing I could imitate her. Mom made that happen. She cleaned houses as a side job and made an agreement with my piano teacher, in exchange for lessons. I was the oldest student. At my recitals, I was always the last to play. Everyone was so impressed, it gave me a sense of pride and confidence. Mom was always supportive and encouraging. She was diligent in making me practice, when many times I would have rather been playing outside.

Coming out of elementary school, I was extremely popular so entering a Jr. High where I did not know anyone, was difficult. High school was also difficult the first year. However, as a sophomore, I went steady with this popular guy, who was a junior. He had a car and a motorcycle, which was "cool." He sang and played the guitar. He was my first boyfriend. Well, that lasted three months. I was heartbroken. During my last two years, I flourished and gained more confidence with my teachers, who liked me and encouraged me to do my best. My favorite subjects were, English, Speech, Photography, Ceramics, and the performing arts, Modern Dance, Choir and Theater. I was also involved in extracurricular activities, such as drill team, where I marched in the Mother Goose Parade a few times, as my family cheered me on. At my first musical audition I sang, "Jesus Loves Me." I believe His name got me the part! I had a boyfriend for those last two years who use to pick me up for school on his 10 speed bike until he purchased a car, which was a great relief. He played basketball, football and tennis. He was a great guy!

My senior year was the best. By the way I behaved, my friends knew I was a Christian. I wasn't yet bold enough to discuss it freely. They, as well, were not into alcohol or drugs. My befalling sin was dancing, which was a sin according to Mom. Of course, it was never provocative or sensual. Dancing for me was fun and exciting. It was a blast going to my high school dances and dancing with football players, who didn't know how to dance. During my junior year, Pastor Court invited Mom and me to visit a college, which was at that time called, California Baptist College in Riverside. It was a great visit and I met some wonderful people, without knowing I would enroll. My passion was music. I loved singing and playing the piano. My senior year, the Lord gave me the desire to become a missionary in music. I wanted to travel the world and sing for Jesus. I wasn't contemplating marriage, children, a career, buying a house or a car. My mind was solely on serving the Lord. However, the Lord had all of that covered, according to His plan for my life. How naïve of me to think in such a manner but, truly, that was my heart's desire.

"Do not lay up for yourselves treasures on earth, where moth and rust destroy and where thieves break in and steal. But lay up for yourselves treasures in heaven, where neither moth nor rust destroys and where thieves do not break in and steal. For where your treasure is, there your heart will be also" (Matthew 6:19-21).

During one Sunday service, as my Pastor gave the invitation, I went forward, dedicating my life to full- time ministry as a missionary. I did not know what that meant or what it looked like. At the end of my high school senior year, I decided to go to California Baptist College. Again, the Lord had His perfect plan for me. I had no money. I hadn't considered going and my boyfriend wanted to get married. I knew I didn't want to marry, especially at age seventeen. Again, the Lord provided a small monthly offering through my Spanish Church. But it was Dad who paid for my education. I was so grateful. I remember him saying how he wanted me to graduate, wearing a black gown. I'm not sure, why and I never asked. I told him that would only happen in college. This is what he wanted. So at age 17, I left home. I was the last child to leave home as I moved to Riverside. In my freshman year I prayed for a great roommate and once again, God provided. She was awesome! Two years later, she married and the Lord blessed me with another roommate who was a pastor's daughter. Little did I know that years later, she and her husband would play a significant role, as I faced the most difficult time in my life.

It was exciting living on campus. This was where I met the father of my children, another athlete. Basketball was his game. I also met Rick Warren and his then girlfriend, Kay. She was beautiful, sweet and soft spoken. On the contrary, Rick was the long-haired, fringe-leather jacket wearing, hippie looking guy, who walked around with his Bible and guitar. He was a passionate preacher, who at times, led the music in our chapel services. I knew that someday, he was going to be a great servant of God. One night, Rick asked me and my roommate if we wanted to go to Taco Tia, a drive-thru that had great bean burritos. I admired Rick's love for Jesus. I admit, I had a little crush on him but it was the Jesus in him that I admired the most. Another time, Rick piled a bunch of us into his seat-less van, to attend a Billy Graham Crusade in Anaheim. It was great fun!

However, at times, I missed Mom and the aroma of home, so for the first year I'd drive home in my VW bug, the car given to me by my brother, Sam. It was a little beat up but I liked the fact that I had my own car. My second year, a gentleman from the college, studying to be a pastor, became the interim Pastor of my church in El Cajon. He played the guitar and together, we would sing unto the Lord. We had a unique relationship. It never developed into a romantic one for he was my Pastor and I highly respected him. After two years, he graduated and left to go to seminary. The night he left, I thought to myself that if I were to marry, I would want to have a relationship such as ours, centered and grounded in Christ.

As soon as I relocated to Riverside, I searched for a church to serve the Lord. I attended La Primera Iglesia Bautista on Sunday and Wednesday nights for Bible study. At times, it was difficult to bypass my studies and go to church midweek. College was difficult for me, but the Lord again reminded me that He would bless my studies if I sacrificed and was obedient. Sure enough, He did. In fact, I did better in my classes! The Lord was faithful. In this church, I got involved and served by playing the piano, singing special music, teaching Sunday school for the youth, assisting in the nursery and directing the Vacation Bible School and the youth choir. Both of my children were also dedicated to the Lord in this same church. Many times, as I was on my way to church, I'd pass by Greg Laurie's church, Harvest Christian Fellowship. Because I was going through a difficult time, in addition to my regular church, I also attended Harvest. As soon as my church was dismissed, I would grab Israel and Lea and take them to Harvest, leave them in the children's church, while I went to worship and receive more of God's Word. My children were amazing! They loved going to church. I raised them, using James Dobson books on rearing children. If I needed to discipline them, which was not often, I would just pull out the wooden spoon and that was enough to get them, back in line. I would, also, listened to Chuck Swindle, on the radio, as he ministered to my heart. At this point in my life, I needed the Lord more than ever, for my heart had been shattered into pieces. In time, God took my fragmented heart and pieced it together, with His loving hand. "The eyes of the Lord are on the righteous. And His ears are open to their cry" (Psalm 34:15). "The righteous cry out and the Lord hears, and delivers them out of all their troubles. "The Lord is near to those who have a broken heart, and saves such as have a contrite spirit. "Many are the afflictions of the righteous; But the Lord delivers him out of them all" (Psalm 34:17-19). "He heals the brokenhearted and binds up their wounds" (Psalm 147:3).

Upon entering college, I thought I knew which field to pursue but the Lord had a different plan for my life. I decided to major in music. While attending my music classes, the Director of the Education Department, an elderly woman who had created such a great reputation for this department, suggested I pursue a major in Education due to the great need for bilingual teachers. This continued for two years. I never dreamt of becoming a teacher. Meanwhile, I was taking voice lessons, singing in choirs, traveling to Northern California, with the Concert Choir, ministering through music. I also joined a bilingual praise and worship team, singing in several churches throughout Los Angeles. It was amazing serving the Lord in this capacity. This is what I loved!

In high school, I always wanted to be on the cheerleading squad but I lacked the confidence. However, as a college freshman, I thought I'd give it a try. Surprisingly, I made the squad and we were pretty good. I didn't care too much about wearing the short skirt, barely above the knees, but short enough for me. The summer after my sophomore year, I was given the opportunity to take a missionary trip to Kansas for ten weeks. What an experience! It was my first time flying, leaving California alone, not knowing what to expect. It was a step of faith, one in which I was more than willing to take. Again, it was Pastor Court and Mom who took me to the airport. As I walked away to board the plane, knowing this was difficult for Mom, Pastor Court prayed aloud, "We put her in your hands." I was excited, my first summer missionary trip! But, I was a bit leery, not knowing what to expect. The first night in Wichita, Kansas, I spent alone, in the home of the Pastor, who was out of town with his family. There was a tornado alert, which was beyond frightening and there were crickets everywhere in the house. I had never experienced such a fierce wind, seemingly, ready to blow the roof off the house. It reminded me of, "The Wizard of Oz." The next day, I met my roommate from Texas, who definitely had the Southern drawl. A week later, we met the Pastor and his family. He would transport us to different churches in the area. I served in five different churches, teaching Vacation Bible School, Backyard Bible Clubs and playing the traditional Baptist hymns in which I was well acquainted. I also witnessed how a faithful Pastor ministered to a small congregation, while another Pastor, who was not as loyal to his wife and children, ministered to a large congregation. It didn't seem right or fair to me. This Pastor even made a pass at me, telling me how I reminded him of a former girlfriend. My roommate and I spent two weeks in his home as I locked myself in the room, trying to avoid him as much as possible. Meanwhile, writing letters to my Pastor, asking for advice and Godly counsel. I watched this man as he interacted with the ladies, sisters of his church, documenting his inappropriate behavior. Before leaving his home, I reported him to the Home Mission Board, which later, dismissed him from his position as the Pastor of that church. This experience was shocking, for I had never observed this with any Pastor. I thank the Lord for the tenacity to stand up for what was right and take action. Again, we all fall short in our weaknesses. But that does not excuse his inappropriate behavior. That is why we need God's grace and forgiveness. Thank God this experience did not ruin my trip.

During college, it wasn't until I bombed my music theory class, and feeling rather discouraged, that I decided to either drop out of college or change my major. Dad encouraged me to stay in college, which was the first time he had given me such sound advice. It meant so much to me that I wanted to make him proud so I changed my major to Education. This was my calling. This was my ministry. God had called me into full time teaching. The public school classroom would become my mission field!

At age 22, after one year of marriage, I graduated. I was the only student in my class who was offered a teaching contract from the Superintendent of the Riverside School District. There was no need to complete an application or resume. At my first interview, I was offered my first teaching contract. Thank you, Jesus! I had never been employed. Living at home, Dad did not allow it. When I was in college, I cleaned houses for an elderly lady and one of my female professors. It was a side job. So, when I looked at the contract and the amount of income I would be earning, I was in disbelief. At the time, there were six schools in need of a bilingual teacher. The Superintendent asked me to choose one. Meanwhile, the principal at the school where I completed my student teaching, was eager to hire me. My choice lasted a couple of weeks as the principle from Liberty Elementary interviewed me and decided she wanted me at her school. She had clout in the district and the school was only five minutes away from my house. Thank you, Jesus!

My first teaching assignment was for a bilingual class with a combination of fourth, fifth, and sixth graders. I was ready to quit the following October but thanks to my full- time aide, I continued. It was extremely difficult but the Lord, once again, held my hand. "For it is God who works in you, both to will and to do for His good pleasure" (Philippians 2:13). "I can do all things through Christ who strengthens me" (Philippians 4:13).

Early on, the Lord had impressed upon my heart to demonstrate His love to all my students. Without mentioning His name, in the public school system, I was determined to do so. I decided I would not allow children of any age to raise my blood pressure, causing me to lose my temper. The Lord gave me patience and a calm spirit as I shepherd them. Many children were already faced with their own family temperaments. The Lord reminded me of His calling on my life and how I was there to minister to all His children, which He had entrusted into my care. "At that time the disciples came to Jesus saying, "Who then is greatest in the kingdom of heaven?" Then Jesus called a little child to Him, set him in the midst of them, and said, "Assuredly, I say to you, unless you are converted and become as little children, you will by no means enter the kingdom of heaven. "Therefore, whoever humbles himself as this little child is the greatest in the kingdom of heaven. "Whoever receives one little child like this in my name receives me" (Matthew 18:1-5).

It was quite evident to the staff, parents, and students that I was a Christian. One year, after school, I shared the gospel with one of my students and he accepted the Lord. Often, I had students knocking on my door, before school hours, asking for prayer. It was glorious!

In June of 1978, I graduated and was hired to teach in a private school, prior to working the following September at Liberty Elementary. I was ecstatic! I knew God had prepared me for this amazing journey. It was never just a job. I loved going to work, knowing I was serving my Lord and it was He, who allowed me to live my passion! Amen?

"And whatever you do, do it heartily, as to the Lord and not to men" (Colossians 3:23).

It was in Riverside where I married at the young age of twenty-one, graduated the following year, purchased a house, had two beautiful children, taught for nine years and survived a painful divorce.

I had my baby boy when I was twenty-five and my baby girl at the age of twenty-nine. Both were born premature, but healthy. Mom loved her grandchildren! The Lord, truly blessed me with the best children. They were well behaved and did not demand a lot of my attention, which was helpful as a single parent. Both were extremely independent. They could entertain themselves, while Mommy napped after a long day's work. They loved Jesus as they were taught Bible stories and sang songs about Him. Every Sunday, my daughter Lea carried her big Bible to church. They both made the decision to accept Christ into their hearts at different times, which made it personal. It was in our home where I said a prayer of salvation with them. At the age of seven, my son Israel, wanted to get baptized. When Lea learned about this at age three, she also wanted to get baptized. So Pastor John from Bethel Baptist, baptized them both at the same time. I can still remember how Lea was so light that her feet kept floating on top of the water. It was precious. Like Mom, I too, became their example, teacher, and mentor but most of all, their Godly mother. I was given a tremendous responsibility, from my Heavenly Father, to do my best in teaching them the ways of the Lord but most importantly to be the best, God fearing, mother.

"But as for me and my house, we, will serve the Lord" (Joshua 24:15b). I loved being a Mommy. One of the first verses they learned and memorized was; "Children obey your parents in the Lord for this is right" (Ephesians 6:1). I love this verse!

"Strength and honor are her clothing; She shall rejoice in time to come. She opens her mouth with wisdom, and on her tongue is the law of kindness. She watches over the ways of her household, and does not eat the bread of idleness. Her children rise up and call her blessed; "Many daughters have done well, but you excel them all. Charm is deceitful and beauty is passing, but a woman who fears the LORD, she shall be praised" (Proverbs 31:25-30).

I did my best to protect them from the things of this world, however, as they grew older, they began to test their boundaries. We traveled down some rough terrain, but thank God, their temptations and decisions did not keep them from His love. Israel and Lea mean the world to me. I love who they've become as adults. They're both hard working, responsible individuals. The Lord has blessed them with great jobs and continues to meet their needs.

After working several jobs, my son finally found steady employment. When Lea was close to graduating from high school, I asked the Lord, how was I going to pay for her college tuition, knowing she wanted to become a teacher. One night, as I was walking around my neighborhood, I asked Him again. He drew my attention to the house He had given me. I refinanced it, and withdrew the entire amount putting it into a college fund, to pay for Lea's college education. Thank you, Jesus! I am extremely proud of Israel and Lea. Since their birth, I have been praying for their soul mates. God provided my son with a beautiful wife, Monica, whom he adores. I'm grateful for her and am proud to call her my daughter. Lea's soul mate is under construction, for the Lord's preparing both of them to share their lives together for His glory!

At age 31, I experienced the most difficult time in my life! Facing a divorce turned my world upside down. It was devastating and the lowest point in my life. On my 31st birthday, my husband took me out, only, to tell me he was leaving.

By the grace of God, Mom, my Pastor and his wife, intervened through prayer. My faith strengthened as I moved forward. "But without faith it is impossible to please Him, for he who comes to God must believe that He is, and that He is a rewarder of those who diligently seek Him" (Hebrews 11:6). The worst part of it was physical separation from my children when they left to be with their Father. I never chose to be apart from them, and now I found myself not having a choice at all. I cried floods of tears every time my babies left. It wasn't fair nor was it right. Jesus said, "Blessed are those who mourn, for they shall be comforted" (Matthew 5:4).

One day when they had returned from their Dad's, I asked about their activities. As they shared, I excused myself from the table, went to my bedroom to break down and cry. I fell to my knees, before the Lord, pleading for Him to comfort me and to hold me in His loving arms. Suddenly, I heard a little knuckle knocking at my door. It was Lea and Israel was standing by. I quickly dried my tears, telling them to come into my room. As they entered, they asked me what was wrong. I lost it, as I began crying, again. Israel hugged me while Lea wiped the tears from my eyes. Neither one of them cried. They were my strength, as God was loving me through my children. He had answered my prayer. From that day forward, I never asked such questions again.

It was a Sunday morning, when I awoke crying, distraught, and depressed because I had seen my husband, the day before, with the other woman. I only wanted to remain in bed and wallow in my despair. I called my Pastor and his wife, asking them to take my children to church. The pastor's wife asked me if I was going to be alright. My response was that I needed to sleep. She was a bit concerned, however, I reassured her that I would not do anything out of character. After they left, I unlocked the doors. I took some prescribed medicine and fell asleep. When they arrived, I pretended to be sleeping. I heard them come into the house and enter my room. They tried to wake me up but I did not open my eyes. After several attempts, they called paramedics. I knew the situation was not out of control, for no one seemed too upset or worried, however, I knew they were concerned. When the paramedics arrived they tried, as well, but I refused to respond. It took everything within me to remain still and unresponsive. I didn't hear my son, who was apparently in the background, watching from a distance, unable to understand what was happening. At one point, it seemed as if the room was empty, when I heard my baby girl say," Mommy wake up." Again, my son and daughter remained calm. Had that not been the case, I would have never taken it this far. After hearing they would have to call the police, I knew I had to open my eyes, for I didn't want to be falsely accused of something I had not done. They asked me a series of questions and told me they were convinced that I was not trying to hurt myself. Having the doors unlocked was one clear sign. I told them I had mistakenly read the medicine bottle and had taken two pills instead if one. This was not true. Again, I lied to them for I had only taken one. Regardless, I was taken to the hospital, to flush out my system. It was an awful experience, but I knew I had brought it upon myself. I did not want to open my eyes to reality. I just wanted to shut out the pain! Somehow, keeping my eyes closed brought forth a sense of separation from reality, which was my way of escape. I knew there were a few false accusations made, but it was the least of my concerns. The heavy burden I had been carrying far outweighed anything else. But the truth of the matter is, that it was all a lie. I lied about being asleep, taking too many pills, and for the first time I am admitting this to everyone. Lying is not my forte and God hates it! Honestly, I had no intentions of telling this story, but the Lord prompted me to tell the truth. Little did I know that my son needed to know what truly transpired. Jesus said, "And you shall know the truth, and the truth shall make you free" (John 8:32). Telling him brought healing and relief. He remembered the experience, quite well. For years he had thought I attempted to hurt myself. Filled with emotion, I apologized, asking him to forgive me for putting him through such an ordeal. He lovingly thanked and forgave me. I don't know why I never brought it up, but I do know the importance of honesty, admitting my serious mistake. Initially, I shared this story with someone else, who was struggling with depression. My intention was to emphasize not secluding oneself and becoming vulnerable to the enemy, for his desire is to kill and destroy.

"Be sober, be vigilant; because your adversary the devil walks about like a roaring lion, seeking whom he may devour" (2 Peter 5: 8).

"By this you know the Spirit of God; every spirit that confesses that Jesus Christ has come in the flesh is of God, and every spirit that does not confess that Jesus Christ has come in the flesh is not of God. And this is the spirit of the Antichrist, which you have heard was coming, and is now already in the world. You are of God, little children, and have overcome them, because He who is in you is greater than he who is in the world" (1 John 4:2- 4). Amen!

Satan desires to separate us from those who lovingly support us through prayer. His mission is to cause us to fall deeper and deeper into despair. For this reason, we should never isolate ourselves. "No weapon formed against me shall prosper" (Isaiah 54:17a). Whatever we're facing whether affliction, oppression or despair, regardless the degree of difficulty, when we give it to God, He restores us back to Him and grants us forgiveness and healing. He knows our pain and suffering. "He is despised and rejected by men, a Man of sorrows and acquainted with grief. He was despised, and we did not esteem Him. Surely, He has borne our griefs and carried our sorrows; yet we esteemed Him stricken, smitten by God and afflicted. But He was wounded for our transgressions, He was bruised for our iniquities; the chastisement of our peace was upon Him, and by His stripes we are healed" (Isaiah 53:3- 5). "He heals the brokenhearted and binds up their wounds" (Psalm 147:3). Glory to God in the Highest!

"Therefore humble yourselves under the mighty hand of God, that He may exalt you in due time, casting all your cares upon Him, for He cares for you" (2 Peter 5: 6, 7).

There is healing in the name of Jesus! There is power in the name of Jesus! There is deliverance in the name of Jesus to break every chain! Hallelujah!

The Lord reminded me that regardless of what I was facing, my children needed me and I needed them. The healing became a moment-by-moment process. I had never experienced such pain in my life. A time in which I questioned my God, asking, "Why?" He gently reminded me of the times He had spoken to me clearly, but I chose not to listen. In spite of it all, I remained faithful to the Lord, knowing He promised to never leave me. For He Himself has said, "I will never leave you, nor forsake you" (Hebrews 13:5b).

"For your Maker is your husband, the Lord of hosts is name." "All your children shall be taught by the Lord; and great shall be the peace of your children" (Isaiah 54:5, 13).

I then decided that Jesus would be the Lover of my soul, He would Father my son and daughter and He and I, together, would raise our children.

After the separation, the divorce not yet final, I left Riverside with Israel, now six, and Lea age two, we returned to Escondido. As a single parent, I hoped to make a fresh start. Prior to the move in June of 1986, I had been looking for a place to live in Escondido. In my search, the Lord led me to newly constructed apartments. I met the manager who advised me to select the apartment I wanted. She gave me the keys, months before we moved in. God is good. I remember the weekends when my children were with their Dad, I drove to Escondido just to sit in my empty apartment and dream of the day I would move in.

My colleagues in Riverside had told me I would never get a teaching job in San Diego County. People can say whatever they want, but God always has the final word. I remember those words spoken by Mom when she spoke to the doctors regarding my brother Sam, as he lay in a coma. Four days later, he awoke from his coma and lived for another five years! Hallelujah! Mom had unwavering faith. It's all about putting your trust in Jesus, for He is God!

"Now faith is the substance of things hoped for, the evidence of things not seen. But without faith it is impossible to please Him, for he who comes to God must believe that He is, and that He is a rewarder of those who diligently seek Him" (Hebrews 11:1, 6).

I knew there was a new school opening in Oceanside that needed a first grade bilingual teacher. I called and scheduled an appointment to meet with the principal and the Director of the Bilingual Program for the Vista Union School District. It was on a Monday. Mom and I had planned to go to San Francisco the following weekend. At the end of my interview, the principal told me he would call if he was interested. I responded, "I'll be waiting to hear from you." I was confident the Lord would give me the job because I knew He would not bring me to this place without providing my needs and those of my children. He is Jehovah Jireh!

"But my God shall supply all your need according to His riches in glory by Christ Jesus" (Philippians 4:19).

Two days after my interview, I had not heard from the principal, so I called again and left a message with his secretary, stating that I was still interested. No response. Again, I called and spoke with the secretary. She told me it was still available and asked if she could return my call. Meanwhile, Mom and I prayed. Shortly after, the secretary called back asking me if I would accept the teaching position for the bilingual first grade class. I was ecstatic! Enthusiastically, I answered, "Yes!"

The Lord provided me a teaching position with the Vista Union School District at a brand new school, Alamosa Park Elementary, which was still under construction. I worked at Alamosa for 24 years and from there, I retired. It was an amazing career! I worked with some wonderful people who, to this day, I've kept in contact. I taught all grades, except Kindergarten. My favorite grades to teach were fourth and second. I integrated music into my daily lessons, also taking on a school-wide chorus and the talent shows which I enjoyed, immensely. Knowing I was a Christian, I had parents requesting to place their children into my classroom. It was wonderful working with them and experiencing the freedom in Christ, to pray for their needs and those of their children. During my last five years, the second graders performed in musical productions. I was able to teach them all how to play the flutophone. It was thrilling!

Both of my children were enrolled in a nearby Christian Preschool. After a year of reestablishing myself and finalizing my divorce at age 33, I purchased a beautiful condo to raise my children. Eventually, I had to take my children out of the private school and place them into the public school system. My son attended the school across the street while my daughter attended Alamosa Park up to fifth grade and eventually transferred to Escondido Union School District. I had always told myself I'd never teach my own children. However, at the time we were on a year-round school schedule and it was imperative to have Lea in my classroom. Due to her independence, she performed well and the same rules applied to her as the rest of the class. There was no partiality. It was a blast having my baby girl in my classroom. She enjoyed my attention while the rest of my class witnessed the motherly side of me.

After being single for seven years, I remarried. Again, I made the wrong choice. The marriage was dysfunctional. It became abusive and intolerable. Something I never imagined that I would be a participant. After two years of being married we separated for seven years.

While, consulting with my pastor, I learned I had Biblical grounds to divorce him. During those seven years apart, my children and I lived peacefully. Eventually, I confronted him about reconciliation however, he wanted to wait another two years. That was not a good sign and I did not agree to it. Finally, we divorced.

Years later, I reunited with a brother in the Lord whom I met at another church. He was a mature Godly man who set a higher standard. I no longer had the desire to choose. Putting it into my Father's hands, I washed mine from having to make that decision. Until then, I choose to remain single.

Mom was extremely selective when it came to my boyfriends but especially a husband. She did not, completely, approve of either. She had her reasons. That should have been a clear sign, however, I thought no one would ever be good enough for me. Before my first marriage, I met a young man who was attending my church in El Cajon, studying to be a pastor. He was from Spain and his name was Jesus, in Spanish. Mom loved him! He was a handsome, Godly man with a great personality. My Pastor had introduced us. What was I thinking? We dated for months and then I eventually reconciled with my future husband. Two weeks before the wedding, Jesus the Spaniard, came to visit me telling me not to marry. He didn't offer marriage but he did want to court me again. I struggled with the idea. I made choices that were not in accordance to His will and Mom's. Both times, the Lord tried to give me a way out but I took the wrong path. I knew what the Bible had said about being unequally yoked but I thought because these men were Christian, I wasn't.

(2 Corinthians 6:14) "Do not be unequally yoked together with unbelievers, for what fellowship has righteousness with lawlessness? And what communion has light with darkness?"

However, both were not, at the time, spiritually mature men of God. I now believe to be equally yoked means to have a husband who is stronger in his faith than me. I made the decisions and suffered the consequences. I take full responsibility for my actions. God's Word is true. "Your word I have hidden in my heart that I might not sin against you. Your word is a lamp to my feet and a light to my path" (Psalm 119: 11, 105). God honors obedience, but does not tolerate willful defiance. It needs to be His way, for His way is what's best. I desired His best but I was not confident, in myself, enough to receive His best.

Jesus said, "I am the way the truth and the life. No one comes to the Father except through Me" (John 14:6). May I clarify? This verse does not say the Virgin Mary, the Pope, Joseph Smith, Buddha, Mohamed, or Kumbaya, is the way to the Father. It clearly states that Jesus, Y'shua, the Messiah, is the ONLY way to the Father. For He is the Son of God, King of Kings and Lord of Lords! Based on this premise, when you reject Christ, you make the decision to live for the gods of this world.

"No one can serve two masters, for either he will hate the one and love the other, or else he will be loyal to the one and despise the other. You cannot serve God and mammon" (Matthew 6:24). Mammon, meaning riches, material wealth, money and possessions.

"Do not love the world or the things in the world. If anyone loves the world, the love of the Father is not in Him."

"And the world is passing away, and the lust of it, but he who does the will of God abides forever" (1 John 2: 15, 17).

Therefore, you have chosen your eternal destiny, which will be in a place separated from God. The Bible refers to this place as hell. "And anyone not found written in the Book of Life was cast into the lake of fire" (Revelation 20:15). When you ask Christ to come into your heart, He writes your name into the Book of Life. Christ offers life everlasting in heaven with Him, for eternity! Hallelujah! Speaking to His disciples before departing, Jesus said, "Let not your hearts be troubled; you believe in God, believe also in Me. In my Father's house are many mansions. If it were not so, I would have told you. I go and prepare a place for you. And if I go to prepare a place for you, I will come again and receive you to Myself; that where I am, there you may be also" (John 14: 1-3).

After living in our condo for eleven years, the Lord put on my heart to make some upgrades. I had it painted, put in new tile and new carpet. It looked beautiful. A year later, He told me to look for a bigger house to take care of Mom. I had a Christian friend, who was my realtor. She assisted me through the entire process. When I found the perfect house, I put my condo up for sale. I listed the sale price as high as I could because there was another condo that had sold for the same price. Meanwhile, I began negotiating for a loan on the house. The first arrivals who had seen my condo, wanted to purchase it that same day. They were also Christian women. We sat down with both realtors, as they made me an offer, prepared to pay the full amount in cash. It wasn't my asking price, so I told them that I would pray about it. Meanwhile, I was also praying for the loan on the new house. The people living there were also Christians. So now there were five Christian women working and praying together, for God's will. One night, as I parked my car across the street from the house, I told the Lord that if He gave me the house, I would use it for His glory. Hallelujah, the Lord heard and answered my prayers! The next day my realtor informed me that the people who were interested in buying my condo wanted it so badly, they were willing to pay the full price. So, I sold my condo a week before I was able to move into my house. We moved our belongings into the garage of our new house while we went our separate ways, until moving day. I told my daughter she would be celebrating her sixteenth birthday in our new home. She too had enough faith to drive her friends by the house, telling them the same. My children were with their Dad the weekend I received the good news. I called Lea and shared how the Lord had answered our prayers. We both cried together, thanking God.

Thus was the beginning of fulfilling the promise I had made to the Lord. He had already put into place those who would benefit from this blessing, beginning with Mom, my family and my beautiful spiritual daughters in Christ: Trisha, Liberty, and Megan. After all the years of living apart, God merged our paths, bringing Mom and me back together again. We celebrated many birthdays and holidays, year after year in our new home, sharing wonderful memories with family and friends. It was the home where Mom would spend the remainder of her life. The place which many called home and truly experienced the presence of the Prince of Peace.

"For unto to us a child is born, unto us a Son is given;
And the government shall be upon his shoulder;
And His name shall be called Wonderful, Counseller,
The mighty God, The everlasting Father,
The Prince of Peace" (Isaiah 9:6).

My purpose in sharing a part of my life's story was to allow you to see the God, whom I serve, and how He always took care of me and my children. He knew what I was going to encounter due to my disobedience. However, my God, never gave up on me and when I was at my lowest point, He not only reminded me of my precious children but of His love and care that would sustain me through those difficult times. God had His hand on my life and continued to bless me, always making provisions for my needs. He desires the same for you. Will you take Him at His Word? "Delight yourself also in the Lord, And He shall give you the desires of your heart (Psalm 37:4).

Jesus Christ is His name! He is my Savior and Lord! He is the only living and true God who is forever loving, gracious, forgiving, merciful, and true to His Word. There is none other and it's for that reason I choose to live my life for Him! "For to me to live is Christ and to die is gain" (Philippians 1:21).

He sacrificed His life on the cross so that you and I could have an abundant life of peace and sustaining joy. I will continue to love and serve Him for the rest of my days and as long as I am here, I will proclaim the name of Jesus, as I await His coming! The longer I am in this world, the more I realize I do not belong here. For this is not my home. Heaven is my home! I long to go home and see Mom again! Knowing this brings a blessed assurance.

Until then, I will continue praying, studying His Word, living my purpose by shining my light, sharing the love of Christ, and the good news of the gospel to those who are lost without a Savior.

"If My people who are called by My name will humble themselves, and pray and seek My face, and turn from their wicked ways, then I will hear from heaven, and will forgive their sin and heal their land" (2 Chronicles 7:14).

"Study to shew thyself approved unto God, a workman that needeth not to be ashamed, rightly dividing the Word of truth"

(2 Timothy 2:15). "Preach the word! Be ready in season and out of season. Convince, rebuke, exhort, with all longsuffering and teaching. But you be watchful in all things, endure afflictions, do the work of an evangelist, fulfill your ministry" (2 Timothy 4:2, 5). Yes, Lord!

"Go therefore and make disciples of all nations, baptizing them in the name Father and of the Son and of the Holy Spirit, teaching them to observe all things that I have commanded you; and lo, I am with you always, even unto the end of the age" (Matthew 28: 19, 20).

"Let your Light so shine before men, that they may see your good works and glorify your Father in heaven" (Matthew 5:16).

Who is this man? Jesus is His name, Son of God and coming Messiah! He is the Great I Am! People, get ready for the Day of Judgment is coming! The King is coming! Praise God, He's coming again!

Jesus speaking, "Then they will see the Son of Man coming in a cloud with power and great glory. Now when these things begin to happen, look up and lift up your heads, because your redemption draws near" (Luke 21: 27, 28).

"And behold, I am coming quickly, and My reward is with Me, to give to everyone according to his work. I am the Alpha and the Omega, the Beginning and the End, the First and the Last. Blessed are those who do His commandments, that they may have the right to the tree of life, and may enter through the gates into the city" (Revelation 22: 12-14).

The First Sign
of a Stroke

Mom was a healthy and active 90-year-old woman. For eight years, she managed to walk up and down the stairs of our home without any assistance. By no measure, was Mom your typical "rocking chair" grandma for she was always quite physically active.

At times, she experienced some memory loss, but for the most part, Mom was mentally sharp. She did not like being alone for too long for she would become lonely and bored. One of her greatest fears, as she exclaimed, was to die alone.

One day in 2008, I arrived home and found Mom lying on the floor in the family room. She was lying on her back with a pillow under her head. When I spotted her, I immediately ran to see if she was alright, asking what had happened. Lying peacefully on the floor with eyes focused on the ceiling, she was unaware of how she got there. As I carefully helped her up, she seemed rather despondent. She had removed her shoes and somehow made her way into the family room, had grabbed a pillow, placed it under her head and was either waiting to die or waiting for someone to find her. There were no symptoms of a stroke nor soreness, bruises, or broken bones. She seemed fine but could not recall the incident. Perhaps, she had taken her shoes off and had slipped on the wooden floor. To this day, no one knows what really happened.

Whatever the explanation, I knew God held her in His arms. Mom talked and walked normally. But two days later, she fell out of bed and was unable to walk independently. Her right hand was slightly limp. Apparently, Mom had suffered a stroke. I immediately took her into the ER where the medical professionals administered a battery of tests and concluded she had experienced two mild strokes. The first had occurred the day I found her on the floor. After discovering this, I wish I had been with her that particular day. I don't know what would have prevailed or if circumstances would have been different, but the thought of not being there for her still hurts.

From this point forward, my life changed drastically. The time had come to move Mom into the bedroom downstairs. This house perfectly accommodated her needs. Mom's bedroom was a short distance from the bathroom and to her chair in the family room. After her second stroke, the doctor suggested placing her into a nursing facility for a week, so she could undergo physical therapy three times a day. Reluctantly, I agreed.

The night I brought her home from the nursing facility, was her first time in her new bedroom. She loved it! The windows were draped with her favorite colored, hot pink curtains, while a colorful bedspread brightened the room. The wall next to her bed was covered with family photographs including one that framed her name. It read, "Josephine," "She shall increase in wisdom," along with the scripture verse; "Be not conformed to this world, but be transformed by the renewing of your minds" (Romans 12:2). As Mom laid in her bed, the wall directly facing her held a picture of Jesus shepherding His sheep. I purposely placed it there to remind her, as she awakened, of His presence and loving care.

That first night, however, would be the first of many difficult nights. She was suffering from dementia and was confused and irritable. There was no pleasing her. Furthermore, her body temperature fluctuated which made her quite uncomfortable. At times, I became extremely frustrated and didn't know what to do. I prayed, asking the Lord to help me and to give me the strength and patience I needed to get through this, knowing she was the one experiencing the worst of it. It was difficult to see her manifest this type of behavior. There were times when she was distant and impersonal with me. Even when I turned on the TV so she could watch the preaching and listen to worship, there was no response. In my mind, I was trying to return to some normality, but to no avail. Things would never be the same again. Witnessing this change in her became extremely difficult for me. But as time passed, Mom became more coherent and responsive, however, her sleeping patterns were inconsistent. Often, she would awaken at 4 a.m.! I would get little sleep and then go to work the next day. It was getting cumbersome and a few times I felt I could not give any more of myself. Assistance from both my daughter and sister brought some relief but for the most part, I was carrying the bulk of the responsibility. It was draining me physically, mentally and emotionally. At this point, I decided to hire additional assistance. The Lord provided three care givers at different periods of time: my neighbor, who was a nurse, a friend and a family member. All were absolutely wonderful caregivers whom Mom loved. Truly, they were heaven sent.

The stroke had left Mom with a slightly limped right hand which she used to feed herself. With her right foot, she was able to walk but with assistance. Her body could no longer balance but there was no paralysis. Her face and speech were not impaired. Thank you, Jesus! Her physical therapist came to the house, twice a week, to help her exercise and strengthen her arms, hands and legs. He also instructed me on how to continue the exercises in his absence. After the therapist's time was up, I continued overseeing her daily therapy. She gained strength and her cognitive abilities improved. Thank you, Jesus! Mom increased her interaction with family and friends. Many times, she became restless while sitting on her chair, and would tell me to get her up to walk. That always brought an overwhelming joy for it was obvious she was determined to maintain mobility. Slowly, she was becoming herself again! It was our God, the Lord Jesus Christ! Thank you, Lord.

As old as she was, she maintained great determination and never stopped trying. Every day, she got out of bed and walked to the bathroom. I would change her clothing, washed her face, brushed her teeth and combed her hair exactly the way she liked it. Mom was very particular about her hair. She didn't like anyone touching it and when she was in a car, the windows had to be up so that the wind would not mess up her hair. She would always dye her hair to avoid the gray. But eventually her crown of glory appeared and it was beautiful! "The silver-haired head is a crown of glory. If it is found in the way of righteousness" (Proverbs 16:31). Finally, I would put on her jewelry, her favorite earrings and necklace, with a slight spray of perfume. Then, Mom would walk into the family room to eat and feed herself with her right hand, until her hand became too weak. She watched her T.V. evangelists and started singing again! Her melodic tunes were the sweetest sounds to my ears for I had not heard her sing in such awhile. I was in awe!

Mom also developed loving relationships with the young ladies from my Life Group Bible Study. She participated in our prayer time and astounded us by the way she spoke to her God. Mom was fully aware of His presence and power. At times, her dementia would interfere and she would become restless but with zeal she proceeded. However, it was a trying time for me as I taught the Bible studies, prepared treats for the ladies and attended to Mom's needs. But God gave me the patience and assurance that He was in control. My loving friend Megan would often intervene and assist me with Mom. It was such a blessing! The daily routine continued for quite some time. Mom was strong and relentless. It was wonderful to enjoy her again! My God is an Awesome God! "Let all the earth fear the Lord: Let all the inhabitants of the world stand in awe of Him" (Psalm 33:8).

Facing Opposition

When a family member is terminally ill and facing death, it strongly impacts the rest of the family, especially when it is a parent. Sometimes it causes division and ill feelings. Emotions are running at high voltage and at any moment there could be a huge explosion. Whether it is guilt, fear, anxiety, or the tremendous sense of loss, the death of a loved one can create discord, dissension and strife. We all come from dysfunctional families to some degree. Most of us have been affected by a bad relationship with a family member. Such negative experiences may have lasting effects if there is no intervention. Denial of this often prevents us from looking deeper within to acknowledge the issue.

It is difficult to rehash the past as it may trigger painful memories. Many attempt to avoid this by taking alternative avenues of remedy by practicing destructive behavior. Without professional and spiritual intervention, dysfunction progresses from generation to generation. Intervention is imperative in breaking this vicious cycle.

I thank the Lord that initially, this was not the case with my family. My sister moved in before Mom experienced her first stroke. Around the same time, my brother also moved in for a short while. Mom was surrounded by her children and grandchildren. We worked together to make the best decisions for her. It was a difficult and trying time for all of us when Mom was experiencing the worst part of her dementia. At one time or another, we all lost our patience due to the frustration of not knowing or understanding what was happening. But more than anything, it was the pain of seeing Mom in this condition which began to stir up such strong and negative emotions.

As I further educated myself regarding Mom's condition, I grew more compassionate, understanding and patient with her. Although it was extremely difficult, by the grace of God, the circumstances evolved into a beautiful and amazing experience, one I would repeat. For all involved, the circumstances with Mom contributed to the pressures of everyday life, especially for one particular family member Accepting full responsibility for Mom created some separation within my family. Again, the negative feelings surfaced from the past, due to lack of intervention. Mom became less active and eventually, was conformed to her bed. Although she never complained, it was difficult for all to see. People deal differently with loss. Some prefer to keep their distance and not confront the matter, while others sacrifice their discomfort to be present with their loved one. Then again, some try to avoid the issue by placing their loved one in a facility, which can handle the situation more professionally but not in a personal manner. To me, the absence of family and friends is sad and bothersome.

It wasn't as difficult for me to see the drastic changes that had affected Mom, since I had been with her from the beginning. Yet at one point, it was rather obvious for she became thin and frail but her countenance was radiant and she was at peace. She looked beautiful!

The explosion I referred to earlier, finally occurred. It was a release of all the toxins that had been fuming for years. The first occurrence was heated with angry words, threats and false accusations. Mom was present, pleading for it to stop. Finally, it did but the damage had been done. I can see why the Bible says in Ephesians 4:29, "Let no corrupt word proceed out of your mouth, but only that which edifies and gives grace to the hearer only." One can never take back ugly words spoken in the heat of anger. In the book of James, chapter 3, it gives warning of a tongue that cannot be tamed, a tongue capable of setting a forest on fire, causing great destruction.

I wholeheartedly regretted my part. When being verbally attacked by a loved one, the first reaction is to lash back. But that is not God's way. Knowingly, I surrendered my actions and responded accordingly to God's standard, however, it didn't come easily. It took some time to get me to a place of true repentance. I was deeply hurt by the things that were said and the actions which were imposed upon me. I took the initiative and apologized for my actions more than once. Although the other party apologized as well, I realized the apologies were not genuine due to the extreme actions conducted repeatedly by this individual.

My first encounter with the Adult Protective Services was frightening and unexpected. I was unaware of what was happening when a representative knocked on my door. After a few questions, I allowed this person to come into my house, which proved I had nothing to hide. After the meeting, I asked what would happen next. The representative assured me that the case would close. However, after three months the case could reopen, should there be another complaint. Sure enough, it reopened 5 more times! Throughout this process, I began asking questions, educating myself regarding the system. The fact that this person was no longer welcome in my home, resulted in further attempts to devalue me and speak ill of me to other family members. Degrading others comes from a lack of self- worth, somehow making one feel haughty.

After several meetings and telephone calls from Adult Protective Services, I questioned my rights and the false accusations directed towards me. When was it going to stop? The authorities were fully aware of Mom receiving the best of care. What were my rights in protecting the both of us?

Threats were made to place Mom into a nursing home, only to have under paid, overworked, strangers provide mediocre care. More importantly, Mom had made it clear to never put her into a nursing home for any duration.

Police officers were at my door, releasing Mom, when I wasn't home. Grant it, this person had the right to visit Mom but did not have the right to disrupt my home by disrespecting her. The police suggested a restraining order. However, I knew it wasn't the right thing to do and Mom would have never agreed to it.

When hospice came onto the scene, there were accusations of starving my Mother. God put hospice into place to defend me, for it was the hospice professionals who informed me regarding Mom's condition, including her appetite. They informed me of not overfeeding her since her body no longer required as much food. Her lack of appetite was normal. After dealing with several calls and threats, hospice informed me they could no longer receive these calls and that I was on my own. Thank you Jesus! I was never on my own because He was always with me.

You are probably thinking why would anyone want to go through such an ordeal? It's already bad enough to experience a loss. Is it worth it? I was torn, hit and whipped inside. It was a hard beating, both spiritually and emotionally. It brought an overwhelming sense of anxiety. It was unbelievable!

Living through this hellish experience, I realized that this was a spiritual war. "For we wrestle not against flesh and blood, but against principalities, against powers, against rulers of the darkness of this world, against spiritual wickedness in high places" (Ephesians 6:12).

These disastrous incidents empowered me to behave in a position of authority against powers of darkness and rise above them by applying God's authority. The efforts to destroy my testimony would no longer disturb me for I knew my position in Christ and I realized the actions on the part of this family member were straight from the pit of hell. This person was in agreement with the powers of darkness. My battle was not with him/her. My battle was with the enemy! When we choose to sin, we make an agreement with the devil. If we don't repent, these demons can consume us and literally destroy us, to the point of death, separating us from God for eternity. Based on the authority of God's Word, I trusted my Lord to go before me and fight my battle. The battle is the Lord's. As He spoke to Moses in the book of Exodus, "The Lord will fight for you, and you shall hold your peace" (Exodus 14: 14). I had nothing to prove to anyone for God knew, I was in good standing with Him. In retrospect, I've asked myself, would I be willing to go through this experience again for Mom? Absolutely! It was worth it all!

This confirms my point made earlier regarding our deficiencies, the lack of love or self- esteem, etc. which we carry from our childhood. These deficiencies do not just disappear. There is a healing process which must take place and in God's time, He will restore healing which will make us complete in Him!

After months of facing this opposition, the Lord finally put a stop to all the madness! Again, restoring peace in our home. Jesus, the Prince of Peace!

But Peter and the other apostles answered and said: "We ought to obey God rather than men. The God of our fathers raised up Jesus whom you murdered by hanging on a tree. Him God has exalted to His right hand to be the Prince and Savior, to give repentance to Israel and forgiveness of sins. And we are His witnesses to these things, and so also is the Holy Spirit whom God has given to those who obey Him" (Acts 5:29-32).

The End of My Career

In the fall of 2010, beginning the new school year, the Lord spoke to me as I prepared my classroom, saying, "This will be the last time." I always thought I would teach for as long as possible. Teaching was my passion and I absolutely loved it! But, the Lord had other paths for me. Since I heard His voice repeatedly, I decided to inquire. I moved in that direction, trusting His guidance every step of the way.

I cherished every remaining minute with all of my students. I had shared with them that someday I wanted to go to Africa to teach the children. Meanwhile, I was enjoying my time with them. It was one of the best years of my entire career-so wonderfully, fulfilling.

In retrospect, I recognized the Lord's plan, as He ordained my five-year-education by placing me into the public school system, which allowed me to retire at a young age. He knew Mom's needs as well as mine. He is a loving and gracious God! It was humbling and honorable to have followed His plan.

Everyone's circumstances are different. However, the Lord knows our hearts. "Delight yourself also in the Lord, and He shall give you the desires of your heart" (Psalm 37:4). He desires to bless all of His children, when we choose to love Him through obedience.

Throughout my life, Mom took special care of me. Now, it was my chance to grant her the same favor. The Bible states if you honor your father and mother, your days will be long on the earth. Mom was the exemplary daughter who took care of both parents. The Lord was faithful to His promise and blessed Mom with 98 years.

I cherished every single day that I was with Mom and thanked God for the opportunity. I grew to love her even more, which I didn't think was possible. I told her several times a day as she always responded, "I love you too, honey." It was beautiful to be right by her side for the remainder of her life.

Retiring allowed me to completely devote myself to her. It was a new season and purpose in my life-one that I embraced wholeheartedly.

I retired in June of 2010 and the following August, my daughter, Lea, moved to Texas to pursue her teaching career. My career had ended, while hers was beginning. Up to this time, I had a helping hand but because I was the one summoned to be Mom's primary caretaker, I knew the Lord would guide me. Lea and I talked and cried about her leaving. She voiced her concerns for both her grandmother and me. But I reassured her of the Lord's care for us.

> "I will lift up my eyes to the hills.
> From whence comes my help?
> My help comes from the Lord,
> Who made heaven and earth" (Psalm 121:1).

We agreed that it was imperative for her to pursue her career. Thank God, I still had Israel and Monica, who took care of Mom while I attended church. Soon after Lea's departure the Lord sent Liberty, my sister in Christ, to come live with us. She was a blessing to both Mom and me. Lea's one desire was to be present at the time of her grandmother's passing. It was granted.

In May of 2012, my daughter returned home and four months later, Mom ascended to heaven. Jesus said, "If you ask anything in My name, I will do it" (John 14:14). He did.

It has been five years since my retirement. I am profoundly grateful for the freedom I have to spend time in His presence, share the gospel message through the love of Christ and bask in the harvest serving my Heavenly Father! I refuse to retire from the calling God has on my life. The harvest in plentiful!

The following June of 2013, after Mom's ascension, I was able to take a mission trip to Uganda, Africa! I thank God for all who supported me both financially and prayerfully, friends and brothers and sisters in the Lord. It was through, Believer's World Outreach Ministry. A large group of us from the Rock Church ventured into this amazing journey, teaching and sharing the Word of salvation to these beautiful and humble people. Someday, God willing, I would like to return to Uganda to teach in one of the orphanages in Masaka and visit my missionary friends at the Calvary Chapel Church in Jinja. Once again, God granted my heart's desire.

Opportunities for Ministry

The Lord meets us where we are and is ready to use the surrounding circumstances for opportunities to serve Him.

Jesus speaking to His disciples gave them, "The Great Commission."

"Go therefore and make disciples of all nations, baptizing them in the name of the Father and of the Son and of the Holy Spirit, teaching them to observe all things that I have commanded you, and lo I am with you always, even unto the end of the age" (Matthew 28:19, 20).

This is what we, as believers in Christ Jesus, are called to do. Regardless of our circumstances, it is imperative to look for those opportunities and quickly act. Looking back, it was evident to me that the countless visits to the ER with Mom, were a great example of this revelation.

Mom's first episode was one evening when my friend, Megan, and I went to the grocery store to get something for dinner. We were gone for less than a half hour. Meanwhile, my daughter, Lea was home taking care of her grandmother. When we arrived, Lea met us at the door crying uncontrollably upset that mom had fainted.

She had already dialed 911 and the paramedics were on their way. I rushed to see Mom as she sat in her chair, limp. I began praying in the name of Jesus, as I called out to her. I continued, "In the name of Jesus!" My first response was to check her pulse to see if she was breathing. Five minutes later, the paramedics arrived. Four to five men walked into my house with all the necessary medical equipment needed to assist Mom. Her blood pressure had dropped but the paramedics were able to get it back to normal. Hearing Mom's voice again was heavenly, knowing that she was still with us. Meanwhile, they had asked me a gamut of questions regarding her health, medications, also requesting the form that documented the family's request regarding resuscitation. For some time, she had been taking blood pressure medication.

The entire experience was nerve wracking. But the Lord was with us. Lea remained a bit shaken up, for it was quite a scare. But she did all the right things and took every precaution. As they wheeled Mom into the ambulance, I was greatly relieved but at the same time frazzled by what had happened. The Lord gave me the strength and faith needed, to trust Him knowing Mom was in His care. As I grabbed my things to rush to the hospital, I gave my daughter a hug and reminded her of how well she handled the situation. Encouraging her, I reiterated that mom was breathing and that she would be fine. As I was driving to Palomar Hospital, only ten minutes away, I began praying to my Lord, telling Him how much I loved Him and thanking Him for restoring Mom. He covered me with His peace and reassured me of His presence in my life. There were no tears, but only a tremendous amount of peace and pure relief.

Upon arriving to the ER and checking in, I was directed to the room where they were holding Mom. She was awake and a bit nervous. I explained to her what had happened and reassured her that she was going to be fine. I stayed with her as she fell in and out of sleep, praying for her all the while. Finally, the doctor came in and explained the battery of tests needed to find the cause of her episode. As a precaution, the doctor decided to keep her over night to closely monitor her heart and vitals. I knew that I needed to stay with her. At that time, she was taking medication for her dementia, so needless to say, she was awake most of the night. It was a rough night for us, however, the Lord reminded me that it was not about me. Mom was the one who always stood by taking care of me even when I needed hospitalization. She was my mother, whom I loved and cherished. There was no way I would have left her alone and I had given her that reassurance.

The next day, family members arrived to visit and inquire about the recent activities. The results of the tests were negative. Anytime you're taken into the hospital, there is always an evaluation of medications along with re-evaluations. Because it had been her blood pressure, the doctor decided to change Mom's medication. Everything else was fine. Thank God again for His faithfulness and His never-ending love.

The fainting spills continued. I began asking the Lord if there was something I was missing in all of this. After the second time, I took my Bible. Reading it to Mom, gave her comfort and strength as the Word of God spoke to her mind and spirit. Since I was a little girl, I've had a heart for the lost. My passion has always been evangelism. So I took my Bible tracks, "Peace with God," by Billy Graham. These tracks are small pamphlets which contain the powerful message of salvation through Jesus Christ. I have discovered that most people respond to this track because most need peace in their lives and many either know or have heard of the Reverend Billy Graham. As I entered the ER, it was full of people in need; the Lord told me to distribute the tracks. But as I waited in line, I began to bargain with the Lord, asking Him if I could check on Mom first. When I approached the receptionist, she told me I would have to continue waiting. Immediately, I distributed the tracks to mostly everyone in the room. When I finished, I sat down keeping a close eye on the clock. Two minutes later, I returned to the desk. Then, I was permitted to go inside. In that waiting room, the Lord revealed to me that there were lives who needed to know the peace and healing that only God brings. Holy Spirit is always at work. While we sit and wait for our circumstances to change, the Lord desires that we do something for those around us who, perhaps, are in greater need of Him.

Again, Mom was fine. Thank you, Jesus! Of course she had to go through the same procedure. I reminisced of all that had happened and realized how God held Mom in His hands. However, there were people all around her who needed Him and this was my opportunity to share the gospel, the good news! I began passing out tracks to the nurses and doctors, sometimes leaving them on their trays. Whomever the Lord placed on my heart at the time. I met one nurse who confessed that He also knew Jesus. It was awesome!

This one particular time Mom had fainted while Megan, whom Mom loved dearly, was now living with us. Her pulse was weak while her color and body temperature had changed. Crying, I called out, begging her not to leave. I asked Megan to make the call and again, we both followed the paramedics to the hospital. God's plan was for Megan to be there. As we waited for the doctor, we overheard a conversation between a patient and the nurse. They were conversing about his amount of alcohol consumption. He was loud and wanted to leave. Megan and I began praying for him. As we continued listening, she expressed her desire to speak with him. Of course, I encouraged her to go, sending her off with a track. She was able to share her testimony, telling this man that at one point in her life, she too was in the same place but Jesus saved her and transformed her life. Again, it was God's perfect timing in motion. He took the track graciously and as he left, thanked her for sharing with him. The entire time, Mom was fast asleep. Do you recognize how God can work through our circumstances? It is never about us, only. God's plan exceeds to a greater number of participants who will be affected, in some way, by His goodness. He desires to reveal Himself to the world. He died for the world and it is through His people, that He will reach the world.

From that point on, whenever Mom had an episode, I looked for opportunities, for I knew it was part of His plan. It was exciting knowing, all the while, that Mom was in God's care. There were many others He sent my way to minister to their needs. Some were friends, whom I hadn't seen in a while. Another one was my alcoholic cousin, who was down the hall from Mom's room. I prayed with him and his nurse.

However, the episodes continued. There were a total of eight visits to the ER. The last time, I asked the Lord, who was I missing. They continued for a reason. There's always a purpose in God's plan. He reminded me of the paramedics. The first thing I did when I arrived at the hospital, was hunt them down to give them a track of salvation. Finally, the episodes stopped. Hallelujah!

After each episode, I wondered what I would encounter, seeing Mom again. Whether there would be any lingering effects due to the lack of oxygen. But each and every time there were no signs! My God is a miraculous God!

"This beginning of miracles did Jesus in Cana of Galilee, and manifested forth his glory; and His disciples believed on Him" (John 2:11).

Medically, it was diagnosed by one doctor as the vagus nerve. When the vagus nerve, which is connected to the brain, is stimulated, the response is often a reduction in the heart rate or breathing. This happens to everyone while baring down, causing the blood pressure to drop. For this reason, many elderly pass away on the toilet or in church. I'd rather be in church!

Someone once asked me, "How do you do it?" As I pondered that question, I realized my answer was simply, unconditional love. In the midst of it all, an overwhelming sense of love empowered me to always put Mom's needs first. Unconditional love can override any circumstance. I was reminded again that in every circumstance, God is always at work, seeking those in whom He loves. He is relentless and He will continue to seek you out. Amen? His desire is for you to know Him. Do you know His love?

Visits to the Nursing Homes

Due to Mom's determination not to live in a nursing home, I honored her request, in spite of a few challenges. After her second stroke, the doctor suggested for Mom to be placed in one, to accommodate her physical therapy. I reluctantly agreed but it was only for seven days.

On the night Mom was transferred from the hospital, I explained to her the timeline of events, while reassuring her I would be with her at all times. I followed the ambulance to the facility to ascertain she received quality care. However, it was extremely difficult for me to leave. Her dementia triggered and she began telling me how badly she wanted to go home. Like a little girl, she began crying and begging me not to leave. I called the nurse for assistance but she was busy with another patient. I decided to stay the night. I went to the front desk, requesting permission, and was told I needed to wait for the Supervisor. After waiting for nearly an hour, I returned to the desk, a bit disturbed, that I had waited so long and no one attempted to respond. By then it was 9 p.m. The nurses suggested that I go to the Supervisor's office but she was not there. As I returned to Mom's room, she continued begging. She wanted to go home. At that point,

I didn't know what to do. I started crying. I was torn. I didn't want to leave her. I contacted my brother and he assured me Mom would be fine and for me to go home. The nurses would have to attend to her. I took his advice and left, deeply upset and crying all the way home.

I made daily visits, took her outside for fresh air and stayed with her as long as possible. After seven days, my siblings went to discharge Mom and bring her home. They were concerned about Mom's appearance, as if she was going to die from the medication administered to her. The doctor had told them to leave her at the facility for one more night for close supervision. When I arrived home from work and learned what had happened, I became extremely irate and was determined to bring her home. The Lord reminded me of how I needed to represent Him in a calm manner.

During most of my visits, I performed the duties of the nurses. A few times, I asked for assistance but no response. It was quite disturbing, to say the least. I knew Mom had to leave this facility.

As I walked into the building, Mom's back was facing me as she sat in her wheelchair eating dinner, wearing a stranger's dirty clothing. I told her I was taking her home and proceeded to gather her belongings. As I walked down the hallway, I spotted a nurse and informed her of what I was doing. She said I needed to get the release from the doctor. I responded, "Regardless, I'm taking her home." She smiled, seemingly impressed. Before I left the room, I asked the patient next door if I could pray for her. She replied that she was a Jehovah's Witness. I told her I believed in Jehovah God, as well. "Trust ye in the Lord forever: For in the Lord JEHOVAH is everlasting strength" (Isaiah 26:4). After my prayer, she thanked me. She had often heard me praying and reading the Bible to Mom and commented on how much she enjoyed it. The nurse returned with the doctor's release and Mom's medications. I thanked her, wheeled Mom out, and never returned.

I must admit that during her last stay in a different nursing facility she was well cared for. Due to our Heavenly Father, she was given a beautiful, clean room, with a couch for her visitors. The nurses were friendly and attentive to her needs. Mom was comfortable during her short stay. However, her desire was to be home and home is where she rested for the remainder of her life. Again, it was God's goodness.

"Surely goodness and mercy shall follow me.
All the days of my life;
And I will dwell in the house of the Lord
Forever" (Psalm 23:6). Amen!

My Second Family

I called upon my Lord, requesting guidance to care for His precious child. He revealed physical signs of Mom's capabilities as well as her weaknesses. Mom loved to eat and enjoyed her daily meals. But as her appetite decreased, I grew concerned. At this point, thanks to my brother Joe, I contacted hospice. It was comforting to know I had his guidance and support. When making such crucial decisions, family is critical. This was our mother and we needed to be on the same page regarding her health and welfare.

In April 2012, shortly before Mom's 98th birthday, I called hospice and met with the consultant regarding Mom's condition. It was an informative meeting, compelling me to commit to their service. The meeting confirmed that hospice was exactly what Mom and I needed. The team consisted of nurses, a social worker and a chaplain who made weekly visits. Little did I know I was about to embark on an amazing journey with these God-sent individuals who would provide the necessary support. Just knowing they would be there for me and my family brought tremendous hope and comfort. Their philosophy for one who is transitioning, is to make the individual feel comfortable, with the least amount of pain so he/she can transition with dignity and honor.

I was now in the company of experts who would guide me through tough decisions. Again, the Lord granted me favor. With His guidance and the expertise and support from hospice, I was able to adapt to Mom's changes. The nurses were attentive to my needs and concerns. I especially loved how the chaplain, unbeknown, read some of Mom's favorite Psalms to her.

Mom also had a physical therapist who came to the house twice a week to walk with her and perform exercises that were conducive to her condition. I watched and learned, knowing I would eventually take over. Mom's nurse was a kind and gracious Christian woman. At this point, Mom was becoming weaker and could no longer stand upright. The nurse asked me why I was still getting her out of bed. In my ignorance, I didn't know how to respond. I thought I was doing the right thing. The nurse gently explained how Mom could receive excellent care in her bed and that it was now time to make this transition for her to remain there. With a hospital bed, it was easier to make this adjustment while Mom remained extremely comfortable. God is good! "And my God shall supply all your needs according to His riches in glory through Christ Jesus" (Philippians 4:19). Amen!

As time passed, the hospice team became my extended family. They even participated in Mom's 98th birthday celebration. We sat her up in bed, gave her a cake with a lit candle and sang happy birthday. She was coherent and delighted that we were present. Although she was not cognizant that it was her birthday, she enjoyed the company and attention. Little did we know this birthday would be her last.

I became a student as day by day, I eagerly learned new things, putting them into practice. Because I'm so inquisitive, I never hesitated to ask questions. My new hospice family was very patient with me. Although at times I thought I was asking ignorant questions, the staff never made me feel inferior. They regularly asked me if I had any questions to make sure I completely understood the chain of events. Granted, at times, they didn't have the exact answer, but always gave me the reassurance I needed. When the time would come for Mom to go to heaven, I wanted to be certain that I had done my very best for her, without any regrets.

Mom spent most of her time sleeping. On several occasions, the nurses entered her room quietly to not awaken her. They frequently commented on how she appeared so sound and peaceful as she rested. One time, a substitute nurse came to our home and commented on how she felt embraced with peace. I told her it was Jesus. Much to my delight, she admitted to being a Christian. She told me that throughout her lengthy nursing career, she had never seen a patient look so at peace. I was amazed by her comment. I shared my thoughts with her regarding Mom waiting for a loved one. I had expressed to Mom that it was OK for her to depart, reassuring her that I would miss her deeply but knowing we would see each other again. The nurse responded, "She's waiting for you and she will know in her heart when you are ready." I began to cry. No one is ever ready to release a loved one but I thought I was as close as I would ever be. God knows the perfect time and He knows the hearts of His children. What a kind, gentle and loving God I serve. He never ceases to amaze me. "For His loving kindness is great toward us, and the truth of the Lord endures forever" (Psalm 117:2).

Mom slept while the nurse completed her paperwork. When it was time for the nurse to leave, she expressed her desire to linger because of the overwhelming peace she had experienced. She was an angel sent from God to give me that message. I never saw her again. "For He shall give His angels charge over you, to keep you in all your ways" (Psalm 91:6).

The social worker was another gift from above. She was available to meet with the family members simply to talk about their thoughts and feelings and to offer support. My brother met with her a couple of times, but I was the one who benefitted the most from our one-on-one sessions. As we conversed, the social worker asked me some soul-searching questions. Often times, I was unaware of the emotions stirring up inside until I spoke with her and poured out my heart and soul. Floods of emotions gushed out as tears ran down my face. It brought an overwhelming sense of relief. At one point, I shared the gospel with her and explained how Jesus was carrying me through this season and that He was responsible for the love I had for Mom.

"To everything there is a season,
A time for every purpose under heaven;
A time to be born,
A time to die,
A time to weep,
And a time to laugh,
A time to mourn,
And a time to dance" (Ecclesiastes 3:1, 2, 4).

The social worker frequently encouraged me and tried on many occasions to give me credit for taking such good care of Mom but I continuously pointed to Jesus. I thanked the Lord for her presence and professionalism. The last time I saw her, she told me I was going to be alright. We hugged and said our goodbyes. Sadly, she did not accept Christ into her heart but the seed was planted. Prayerfully, someday she will recognize who He is and how much He loves her.

The last six months of Mom's life were completely comfortable and peaceful. She was never in pain, taking no medication and all of the symptoms, which could have exacerbated, never did. I could see how much Jesus loved her and granted her favor. Her life was in His hands.

At this point, I was Mom's primary caregiver. Although Israel, my daughter-in-law Monica and my brother Joe lived nearby, Mom was in my care 24/7. It was an exciting challenge because I knew God was motivating me to provide top-quality care for His precious child. I had to surrender mentally, physically and most importantly, spiritually to give my all for her. What was the end result? The greatest fulfillment of all! I experienced tremendous joy and love for Mom. She took care of me, taught me the way of the cross and loved me. Now it was my honor to do the same for her and the Lord had prepared the way. He gave me a career, allowing me to live my passion in ministry for 32 years. Furthermore, He allowed me to retire at the perfect time so I could devote myself completely to care for the one who once completely cared for me.

You may be thinking, "That worked for you but not everyone is able to with a job, family and other responsibilities." Honestly, had I known that someday I would experience what I did and the tremendous responsibility, I probably would have had the same thought. Humbly, I acknowledge that I would not have been so selfless if it were not by the grace of God. He prepared me for this journey by guiding me towards my career, ministry and family by giving me the strength needed to provide care for Mom the remainder of her life. Jesus promised that He would not only be with me but that He would carry me when I became too weary to move on. "Come to Me, all you who labor and are heavy laden, and I will give you rest" (Matthew 11:28). He is the strength of my life! "I will love You, O Lord my strength. The Lord is my rock and my fortress and my deliverer, My God, my strength, in whom I will trust"

(Psalm 18:1, 2). This thrills my soul! I often wondered how my life could exist without Mom. The thought was inconceivable and too devastating. She was my rock, my closest friend, my Mama, the love of my life. The Word of God, the Bible, is infallible and incapable of error. Every word is true and I am living proof. God is faithful to His Word! Great is Thy faithfulness!

Mighty is His name! God showed me that I could do all things through Him. He taught me how to nurse Mom by providing the proper tools: joy, vigor, tenacity and His unfailing love.

CHERISHED MOMENTS

Every morning, as I awakened, I patiently waited to hear a sound from Mom. As soon as I heard her cough, clear her throat or yawn, I became overwhelmed with relief as I thanked the Lord for another day with her. I recognized how life, especially hers, was precious and how much I cherished every moment with her. Mom and I spent much of our time discussing heaven, our eternal home. We marveled over its beautiful description in the Bible and her eventual reunion with her family and friends.

As I often read the Bible to her, she quoted her favorite Psalms, word for word. One of them was Psalm 23: The Lord is the Shepherd of His People.

A Psalm of David:

> The Lord is my Shepherd;
> I shall not want. He makes me to lie down
> In green pastures;
> He leads me besides the still waters.
> He restores my soul;
> He leads me in the paths of righteousness
> For His name's sake.

Yea, though I walk through the valley of the shadow
Of death, I will fear no evil;
For you are with me;
Your rod and Your staff, they comfort me.
You prepare a table before me in the presence
Of my enemies;
You anoint my head with oil;
My cup runs over. Surely goodness and mercy shall
Follow me all the days of my life;
And I shall dwell in the house of the Lord
Forever.

I have been told, when loved ones are ready to depart this world, they begin disconnecting with those in the physical world, and reconnecting with their loved ones in heaven. Mom was definitely transitioning. In fact, I remember the time I went into her bedroom when she waved her hand, signaling me to leave. I felt a bit rejected. Several times, I heard her conversing to her parents, brother and her son, Sam. On one occasion, when I asked to whom she was speaking, she replied, "Oh, that lady." I asked what the lady looked like but she could not respond. Another time she asked me, "Who is that woman sitting on my bed?" She would frequently, call out to her mother saying, "Mama, I'm here. Come and take me with you." There were times, I overheard her talking to children. Smiling, she would look to one side of her bed and address each one as, "Honey." During her child bearing years, Mom had miscarried two children so perhaps she was conversing with them. On another occasion, she shouted out to these men. When I asked her what was wrong, she told me she had seen three men and she thought one of them was her Father. She shouted, "Dad is that you? Where are you going?

Come back for me! Come back!" She asked me if they were coming back. I answered, "Yes, they are." She asked, "How do you know?" I answered, "I just do." This was reassuring, giving her peace of mind. Initially, I thought of the Trinity, Father, Son, Holy Spirit, and then I thought perhaps angels preparing for her arrival.

I often asked her if she wanted to go to heaven and she always responded, "Not yet." Her answer surprised me as I always thought her desire was to be with the Lord and her family. She often asked me if I would accompany her. She asked, "Will you go with me?" I promised her that I would go later. But Mom was never satisfied with my response. As her homecoming drew near, she asked this question several times a day. I believe Mom had an awareness that we would be separated for a time. But the week before her ascension, a rush of emotions came over me as I cried effusively. I went to her bedside, laid my head on her chest and told her how much I loved her and how I would terribly miss her. Lifting her left hand, she began stroking my hair and told me not to cry. I told her I wanted to go with her. She listened as she continued stroking my hair. I loved Mom's gentle touch. When my tears ceased, she said, "No, you cannot come with me now but I will come back for you later. Honey, I know you will be sad but don't be sad for long." The one time I wanted her to say she wanted me to go with her, she didn't. It was then that I knew she was ready to leave.

Close to the time of her departure, Mom told me she was ready. She said she felt different and that something was happening. She held my hand, tightly, as I sang to her. At times I tried to pull away, gently, but she refused to let go as if she didn't want to leave. An hour later, she released my hand. Again, I told her she was going home. I began describing the beauty of heaven, with its pearly gates and streets of gold, and her new body, free from aging! Reminding her of the homecoming her family was preparing in her honor but most of all her Savior! Again, she continued asking me if I was going with her and if I would come soon. Then she said, "Ruthie," the name she called me when I was a little girl, "Are you here?" I told her I was and that I would not leave her side. We then kissed for the last time. She said, "Okay, I will go. Take me to the cross, take me to the cross." Then suddenly, she yelled, "I want to go to a restaurant!" I told her, "Mom, you'll feast in heaven!" She continued, "I want to go outside, take me outside! I want to play the piano!" I said, "You'll play in heaven!"

Mom's vision had faded as a result of her stroke but I was not aware of the severity until she looked directly into my eyes and said, "I can see you, thank God, I can see you." The Lord allowed Mom to see me, one last time, before taking her home. He is such a gracious and loving God. How awesome is He?

A week later, Mom entered the gates of heaven, feasting at the table prepared for her, with the King of Kings and Lord of Lords, walking the streets of gold with her loved ones, singing and playing a heavenly song of praise, unto her God! Hallelujah, Thine the glory, revive us again!

I'm not one to visit cemeteries to place flowers on grave sites because I know it is a place for the dead. I realize, for many it is a memorial. But I remember the many times Mom had told me how her Mother did not want flowers once she was gone. She desired them when she was living. Mom felt the same. She loved flowers so I showered her with them while she was alive. But now she is gone and she's not in the grave. She's alive! She is in heaven! Up till now, I have not returned to her grave site. I don't know if I ever will. But until then, I choose to remember Mom every day but especially, on September 18th, as my family and I continue meeting together to share beautiful memories, in celebration of her life!

A Glorious Day

We are called to invest in the lives of others, especially those closest to us. Life moves tremendously fast. It is time to reprioritize the day. "This is the day the Lord has made; we will rejoice and be glad in it" (Psalm 118:24).

It was the morning of April 2, 2012, a special day for those whose lives would be touched by Mom's love. Due to her dementia, there were days when Mom said very little and could not remember anyone, including me. Yet other days, she was coherent and responsive. Those days were rewarding as she engaged in conversation, as if her dementia was nonexistent. This was one of those days.

As I lifted her from the bed, to a sitting position, she was in a talkative mood. As we spoke, I noticed how she recalled several names of family members. The Lord impressed upon my heart to call them. I began, with my brother and sister. Mom recognized them immediately as she carried on a pleasant conversation with them. Next, I called her grandsons. Recognizing who they were, she called them by name. Two of them lived in Oregon. She asked when they were coming to visit her as they laughed with joy hearing their grandma's voice again. Mom also shared a special time with Charlene, my nephew's wife, laughing as they conversed. She left messages for those who were unavailable. Some in which had been saved, to serve as a lovely reminder of her. Then, I called my cousin Margie, not knowing it was her birthday. During their conversation, Mom recognized her voice and wished her a happy birthday! It was amazing! God is amazing!

What a special gift the Lord had given my family. For some, it would be the last time they'd ever hear her voice again. She ended every conversation by saying, "I love you too, honey." It was so sweet. She loved her family.

We never know what a day will bring. Perhaps distress and oppression or joy and complete fulfillment. But we can rest assured, as God promises His children.

"Oh taste and see that the Lord is good; Blessed is the man who trusts in Him!" (Psalm 34).

"Oh give thanks to the Lord, for He is good! For His mercy endures forever" (Psalm 118:1).

People are His priority and they must be ours as well. There is nothing in this world that can compare to the precious lives of individuals. The gift Mom had given to her family, was another reminder of God's love demonstrated to the world through the gift of His son, Jesus.

Jesus speaking, "These things I have spoken to you, that My joy may remain in you, and that your joy may be full."

"This is My commandment, that you love one another as I have loved you."

"Greater love has no one than this, than to lay down one's life for his friends" (John 15:11-13).

The concept of agape love, unconditional love, is inconceivable. It compels me to love Him even more. He is the Gift that I will always cherish. I will forever be thankful to Jesus for giving me Mom and I will forever be thankful to Mom for giving me Jesus! I stand in awe of His love!

We take life for granted along with the people whom God has placed into our lives. This world does not accommodate God's priorities. We ought to compare the things of this world, which may be of great importance, and examine how they compare to God's plan. He desires that we invest in relationships with family, neighbors, community, those who are in our sphere of influence, making the best of our time. "See then, that you walk circumspectly, not as fools but as wise, redeeming the time, because the days are evil" (Ephesians 5:15, 16).

"But when He saw the multitudes, He was moved with compassion for them, because they were weary and scattered, like sheep having no shepherd." Then He said to His disciples, "The harvest truly is plentiful but the laborers are few. "Therefore pray the Lord of the harvest to send out laborers into His harvest" (Matthew 9:36-38).

We are spiritual beings and there is life after death, everything else in this world, will perish. Jesus said to her, "I am the resurrection and the life. He who believes in Me, though he may die, he shall live. "And whosoever, lives and believes in Me shall never die" (John 11:25, 26). Do you believe this?

For those of you who have not yet made the decision to accept Christ as your personal Savior, there is no other life but in Him.

"That if you confess with your mouth the Lord Jesus and believe in your heart that God raised Him form the dead, you shall be saved. For whosoever calls on the name of the Lord shall be saved" (Romans 10:9, 10, 13).

He gave His life so that you could have life. This is the abundant and everlasting life! You can live forever with your Creator. The choice is yours. Life is but a vapor, here today and then gone. "Lord make me to know my end, And what is the measure of my days, that I may know how frail I am. Indeed, You have made my days as handbreadths, And my age is as nothing before You, Certainly every man at his best state is but a vapor" (Psalm 39:4, 5).

Mom lived 98 years, waiting to be raptured for that was her desire. When I reflect on her long life, it seems to have passed so quickly. But, Jesus reminds me that someday, soon, we will reunite. What a glorious day that will be! This is a promise He made to the world. He is a loving God who does not force His love upon you but desires to pour out this love to you. When you receive His love, you become His friend!

"A friend loves at all times" (Proverbs 17:17a).
"God demonstrates His love for us that while we were yet sinners, Christ died for us" (Romans 5:8).
"For by grace you have been saved through faith, and that not of yourselves; it is the gift of God, not of good works, lest anyone should boast" (Ephesians 2:8, 9).

He, anxiously, waits for you. What will you do?

Mom's Final Hours

On the morning of September 17, 2012, Mom awakened with hoarseness in her voice. Immediately, I called Hospice. The nurse arrived shortly and instructed me to keep Mom's head propped up with a pillow and said to contact her if there were any changes.

Mom slept most of the day. But as the day turned into evening, her voice worsened. This was not typical. As she spoke, her voice became faint. Lea also noticed that her breathing had changed. In my heart, I knew the time had come for Mom's ascension to heaven. Lea called Israel and Monica, my daughter-in-law. They shortly arrived, fully aware of the circumstances. We sat with her, as I read from her Bible: Psalms 23. Peacefully, Mom fell back to sleep.

Later that evening, Mom was awakened by her cough. As Lea and I went to her bedside, we recognized the physical signs of her departing spirit. My daughter had to leave the room, for it became too difficult. Again, I called the nurse. Mom told me to pray for her. I prayed as I held her hand, telling her again how much I loved her, thanking her for being my mom, and reassuring her of my presence. I reminded her that she was going home to be with the Lord. As she lay comfortably, I played the CD my brother had recorded for her, with all her favorite hymns she once played and sang in church. The room was filled with the presence of God. Standing beside her bed with outstretched arms, I began worshipping the Lord. I sang and sang, "Amazing Grace," "The Old Rugged Cross," "Just As I Am," and "What a Friend We Have in Jesus," knowing she could hear me. I sang her favorite Christmas song, "Oh Holy Night." The nurse had not yet arrived, so again I made the call. Apparently, he lost his way, but I knew it was the Lord's plan for us to spend those last few moments, together, alone. God had given us that special time, moments in which I will cherish for the rest of my life. In retrospect, the Lord had given me ample strength for both of us. There were no tears, no sadness, no anger, no disappointment because Almighty God, the Prince of Peace, our Heavenly Father was present, holding Mom while lifting me up with His righteous hand. My God!

By the time the nurse arrived, Mom's body had become weak and limp. I had never met this male nurse. He was rather annoying, as he made untimely jokes. We turned Mom to her side, making her more comfortable. He then suggested giving her a small amount of morphine, which I questioned, knowing she was not in pain. He explained it would help her breathing. At that point, I suggested using the respirator in her closet, anything to make the transition easier. He finally settled down and sat in a chair next to me. I stood at the foot of her bed, asking him how long she would be in this condition. He didn't know. After talking with him, I learned he also was a Christian and had experienced a loss in his family. It was now 3 a.m. As I stood there, I asked the Lord to not allow her to be on that machine for a long period of time. The nurse dismissed himself, as he reassured me that he would be in his car completing forms, if I needed him.

I went upstairs, grabbed a blanket, pulled up mom's chair in her room, placed it beside her bed, and held her hand, which was now void of life. Again, the room was filled with the presence of God, for all I could feel was His peace. Mom too, remained at peace. I looked at her frail, weak hand as I held it and was reminded of how it once had life and how that hand played the piano, turned the pages of her Bible, and prayed for her family. I remembered when her hands used to comb my hair, as a little girl, and scratch my back. The touch of her hands rubbing my head brought so much comfort and now, it was lifeless. Holding her hand, I sat with her through the night, talking about heaven and how someday we would be together, reminding her of her Mama, who was waiting. But most importantly, I reminded Mom of her Creator who would be there to welcome her into His Kingdom.

I waited, before calling the family, to let them know of her condition and how she was now on the respirator. My daughter was upstairs while my friend, Megan, was in her room, fast asleep. Around 6 a.m., I called my brother, Joe, who called the rest of the family. Two hours later on September 18, 2012, as I rested my head on Mom's chest, her breathing ceased. I touched her heart, looked for a pulse in her neck and placed my finger under her nose. There was no beat, no pulse, and no breath. She was gone. I could not believe it. I woke up my daughter and told her Mom was home. I called Israel and Joe. Shortly after, I called my sister. As she and I spoke, we both cried uncontrollably. As I began sharing the details, tears streamed down my face. It was comforting for me, to share that moment with her. I then called our former Pastor, Lonnie Chavez. Mom loved him and his wife, dearly, as he pastored our church in El Cajon. He had visited her prior and had been preparing for her memorial.

When I returned to Mom's room, I removed the respirator, kissed her on the forehead, and again told her how much I loved her. As I gazed upon her, I remembered how she was always afraid to die alone. I realized she never had reason to fear. Before her body was taken, I cut a piece of her hair, crown of glory, to capture the essence of her beautiful fragrance.

"The Lord is my light and my salvation; Whom shall I
fear? The Lord is the strength of my life; Of whom shall
I be afraid? (Psalm 27:1)

God had His perfect plan for her. He knew how much we loved each other and He had given me the privilege, to be with her up to her very last breath. Not only was I able to tell her, confidently, that I would take care of her for the rest of her life, but now it had become a reality. Wow! Rarely, is one able to tell anyone those words of confirmation. But the Lord gave us both that special gift! Thank you, thank you, thank you, Jesus! What an honor! Humbly, I am forever grateful to Him.

My last thought was that no one should have to die alone. Every night, for months, I left a light on for Mom. But that evening, I finally turned it off. Her room remained dark and silent. As I had grabbed her pillow, I walked up the stairs into my bedroom. I had not slept with a pillow in years. As I laid my head down upon Mom's pillow, I fell fast asleep and slept the entire night. When I awoke, the Lord reminded me how this too was the same manner in which Mom had rested her head upon this pillow, peacefully. But this time, hallelujah, when she awakened, she saw the Light: Jesus, the Son of God!

"Who is this King of glory? The Lord strong and mighty,
The Lord mighty in battle.

"Who is this King of glory? The Lord of hosts. He is the
King of glory!
(Psalm 24:8, 10)

Praise be to the Lamb who sits on the throne! Then Jesus spoke
to them again, saying, "I am the light of the world. He who follows
me, shall not walk in darkness, but have the light of life" (John 8:12).
She listened as He spoke these words, "Well done, good and faithful
servant, you were faithful over a few things, I will make you ruler
over many things. Enter into the joy of your Lord" (Matthew 25: 21).
Ten thousand hallelujahs!

"I have fought the good fight, I have finished the race, I have kept
the faith. Finally, there is laid up for me the crown of righteousness,
which the Lord, the righteous Judge, will give to me on that Day,
and not to me only but also to all who have loved His appearing" (2
Timothy 4: 7, 8). Mom is home! Oh, how I long to see her again!
But until that day, I will faithfully follow her example to our God!

Since She's Been Gone

Two years have passed since Mom ascended to be with the Lord. Time passes, quickly. I thought Mom would never pass by physical death, for she had often said she was waiting for the rapture. God blessed her with a long life. She had shared some things with me that I never understood until now.

Mom remained single for the remainder of her life. For quite some time, she lived alone. Now, after all of these years, I also live alone. I know at times she was lonely but never admitted it. She kept herself busy, always on the go. I don't know if I will remain single for the rest of my life but I am certain I will never be alone. Jesus fills my longing and satisfies my soul and when I am sad, He's right beside me.

Years ago when my older brother passed away, Mom told me life would never be the same without him. At the time I didn't understand, but I fully understand now. You see, to this day, I am missing Mom. How I wish I had one more day with her. For I desire to hug her one more time and kiss her cheek, hold her hand and comb her hair one more time. I want to hear her laugher, just one more time. I want to hear her sing and play the piano one more time. I desire to feel the gentle touch of her hand.

I had many opportunities to love and serve her. However, when I realize this will never happen again, it causes a deep sadness within my inner being. Mom was correct – my life will never be the same without her. But the fact of the matter is unbelievable for Mom is gone but I will see her again! Until then, I will carry on her legacy with a deeper understanding and heart felt compassion for the lost. Thank you, Mama.

SOLEMN MOMENTS

During my quietest moments, I reflect on my memories of Mom. I miss the precious moments we shared. I miss her terribly. She knew I was with her until she took her last breath and God granted her that assurance to rest in Him.

My heart fills with emotion when I think about her. I miss you Mom! As I look at the piano she once played, I recall the many times she played and sang unto the Lord. I miss the sound of Mom clearing her throat, even though at times it was annoying. Any sound coming from her room was comforting, but now I only hear the sound of silence.

As I sit in her recliner, I recall how she often fell asleep so comfortably. Now, as I stare at her chair, it remains cold and empty. It lacks Mom's warmth.

Since Mom's passing, her clothes remain in her drawer, while the rest hang in her closet. My attempts to remove her clothing have failed, I realize there's no reason to, for they leave the scent of her presence. However, the sweet scent is slowing fading.

Some may think this is crazy! For me, it's not crazy. It is comforting. It's sweet. It is Mom. Someday, I will do what is necessary. But for now, I choose to hold on, tightly, to her memory.

A Visit with My Cousin

Fifteen months after Mom ascended to heaven, my cousin Cynthia became extremely ill due to a lifetime of abuse and has since gone home to be with the Lord. But during her illness, she had completely surrendered her life to Jesus, trusting Him wholeheartedly. Meanwhile, she was on fire for God, witnessing to everyone possible. Even as physicians and nurses entered her hospital room, she was quick to share the love of Christ. It was an exciting time in her life for she had finally recognized and fully understood the goodness of God. She shared with me her desire to raise her grandchildren and great grandchildren in the admiration of the Lord but her time had come to an end.

During her transition from the hospital to her home, Cynthia was placed into a convalescent home. On the day of my visit, she was taking a stroll with her walker, welcoming me as I drove into the parking lot. It was exciting to see her out of bed, let alone walking. I recall walking in the garden, reminiscing the good times from the past. She often requested my visit so together, we could read the Bible and pray. Regardless of her physical condition and liver cancer, she was enthusiastic about the Lord.

We walked into a room designated for visitors. It was warm and inviting. Pictures hung against the beautifully painted walls. On one side of the room was a huge aquarium while on the other stood a grand piano. Sitting down, I played a few notes to the classical, Fiera Lisa. Had I known there was a piano, I would have come prepared to entertain my cousin, along with other guests.

After settling down, this beautiful and lovely, woman walked into the room, dressed to the tee with her matching jewelry and cosmetics while her hair was tied up into a perfect bun. As she approached us, we introduced ourselves. Her mind was sharp as she spoke eloquently. She discussed her lack of comprehension as to why her family had placed her in such a setting, explaining how they had moved her from another site, closer to them. However, since she had been in this new location, her family had not visited her. She was disappointed. My heart went out to her as I thought how I would have wanted to take care of her. As she sat next to us, she listened as I read the Bible. After a few minutes, she stood up and complained about her back pain. I asked if I could say a prayer and she agreed. She then walked over to the fish tank, simply to stare. She was still within ear shot of hearing us. As she prepared to leave, we reassured her of Christ's love and sent her off with a blessing.

This scenario reminded me of the many parents and grandparents who are placed into these care facilities without input in the decision-making. The need to be surrounded by familiar voices of people who love them, is imperative in an environment that is conducive to their health and well-being. Again, I was reminded of the tremendous blessing the Lord had given me.

I have a special place in my heart for the elderly. When I was a child, our church made regular visits to share the love of Christ by reading the Word, sharing songs and giving them a warm hug or handshake. The touch of another human is powerful and effective in the healing and aging process. One time, as I went to shake this lady's hand, she wouldn't let go. She held on, tightly, not wanting me to leave. Someone had to literally pull me away. It was a bit frightening, as a child but I grew to love these people dearly. As a teenager, our youth groups would also visit and as an adult teaching the youth, we remembered to minister to the elderly. They always welcomed our return for we were family to them. I often felt a special bond with these beautiful, warm and happy people. They truly blessed my life.

I'm fully aware of circumstances which prevent family members from providing care for loved ones and their only option may be to place them into a nursing facility. However, our daily duties often become overwhelming, keeping us in the state of business, forgetting how much we are needed and wanted by our family members. The acronym for BUSY is, Being Under Satan's Yoke. He tends to keep us distracted by things of lesser value. It is a matter of prioritizing. As children of God, we are to obey and honor our parents. At the end of the day, what/who matters the most?

As a word of encouragement, stay connected. Keep in touch and bless those around you; the lost, the body of Christ and especially your family who love and need you. Nothing else should take priority.

My Home

When Mom was in her eighties, she began forgetting things that were detrimental such as turning off the oven or the burners. It was at that time the Lord impressed upon my heart to look for a 4-bedroom house. Thankfully, I found the place which was not only perfect for Mom, and my children, but it was also my dream house.

Considering the several people who had lived in this house, I saw it as a pure blessing. Mom was the first to move in. Following her, throughout the years at different times, were all my siblings, other friends and family members and three beautiful, young ladies, Trisha, Liberty, and Megan from my church whom I had the privilege to mentor, in the Lord. I was given a tremendous opportunity to share God's blessings with others. In the book of Acts, Paul writes to the Ephesian elders of the church. "I have shown you in every way, by laboring like this, that you must support the weak. And remember the words of the Lord Jesus, that He said, "It is more blessed to give than to receive." It was a wonderful season!

Departing my home after 14 years, however, was not easy. I informed my lender of my retirement and requested a loan modification. After five attempts, I was denied and could no longer afford the mortgage. The bank was unwilling to work with me even though, up to my Mom's passing, I had never missed one payment. I hired an attorney to challenge this issue in court. It took two years. During this period, I paid less than $1000 to live in my home. Once again, God was moving on my behalf. However, I was not ready to vacate my house. In the meantime, I prayed for God's continued assistance. I told the Lord that I did not wish to leave. However, the court denied me again. This was difficult to accept but I trusted God. I knew He had a plan and was hoping it coincided with mine. Nevertheless, I put this matter into His hands and detached myself.

"Trust in the Lord with all your heart, and lean not on your own understanding. In all your ways acknowledge Him, and He shall direct your paths' (Proverbs 3: 5, 6).

To avoid a foreclosure, I was advised to pursue a short sale. That transaction lasted six months. During that time, I wasn't paying a mortgage. I was living in a 4-bedroom house, free! Several interested buyers came to view my home. Ironically, I was the one giving the tour. The bank, finally, accepted one of the offers and my dream house sold. When I received the call that I had to leave in 30 days, I was sadden as I began to cry. I asked the Lord, what was I to do and where was I to go? His response was to be still. This was not what I wanted to hear but I obeyed, trusting in my God. He went before and prepared my path.

"Preserve me, O God, for in You I put my trust."

"You will show me the path of life, In Your presence is fullness of joy, At Your right hand are pleasures forevermore" (Psalm 16:1, 11).

As I prepared for my move, I shared the love of Christ and prayed with those who came to my garage sales. Some were believers and others were broken people. I prayed for a gentleman who had lost his job and needed to provide for his family. Another women whose husband had an extramarital affair, leaving her and their daughters. I felt her pain. Throughout this ordeal, I realized how much the world needs Jesus. He desires to take as many lives to heaven as possible. I vacated that house, thanking and praising Him for all the great memories and for allowing me to share His blessings.

God is good! He allowed me ample time to mourn Mom's passing and provided healing for my soul. I lived in my house for 2 1/2 years, paying little to nothing. By that time, I was prepared to depart. God knew what was best for me. When I reentered Mom's room, I removed her clothes from the closet and dresser and packed her other belongings. It was a task that I was able to accomplish with ease. Thank you, Jesus. I was now prepared to leave and begin the next chapter in my life. The Lord gave me peace and strength through this time. God knew what I needed and wanted and He granted me both. More importantly, other lives were touched and blessed throughout the process. I was overjoyed to have lived in that house and to have participated in His ministry. He was gracious and loving throughout the entire ordeal. How could I have felt any differently?

Two weeks had passed when I returned to the house to retrieve some remaining items. Silence permeated the house. It was then, the Lord reminded me that home is where He resides and within the hearts of those who love Him. It is true. My current home bears the presence of Almighty God with His peace which surpasses all understanding. It is now the place where, once again, I can call home.

Moving On

Currently, I am living in my new home. My move was in the month of November. Relocating before the Christmas holidays is not the best time to move but God's timing is always perfect. This holiday season was not the same as previous years. As I reflected on my childhood, and even as a young mother with children, I recall how our family gathered to celebrate Christmas. Not only was this year completely different, but for the first time in my life, I am living alone. I'm not lonely for I know that Jesus is with me. Yes, I long to be with Mom and I get emotional because I want to go back and spend more days with her. But that's not possible. Her time with me on this earth has ceased. It is finished. Just like the words that the Lord Jesus spoke as He hung on the cross. His purpose on this earth was completed.

As I ponder the memories in the house in which I once lived, I think about my relationship with Jesus and how my days are counted. What am I going to do with the rest of my life? In my deepest despair, He reminds me of His presence which always brings comfort.

This is a season of new beginnings. It can be difficult to leave the past behind and move forward, but this is my calling. God has called me to be His ambassador, His hands, feet and mouthpiece.

"Now then we are ambassadors for Christ, as though God were pleading through us: we implore you on Christ's behalf, be reconciled to God" (2 Corinthians 5: 20). I am called to live for Jesus! He is my purpose. I am nothing without Him for He is my all! I could have never survived my struggles without Christ in my life. It would have been too painful and devastating. How could I go on without Mom? She was my rock, my best friend, my Mama. But God is faithful and forever present. You can also experience His love and grace by asking Him to forgive you of all your sins, inviting Him into your heart, believing in His Word and surrendering your life to Him, giving Him full control.

The cords in my family which were broken are beginning to mend. Hallelujah! The Lord is restoring healing. My prayer is that our family will reunite, once again, to celebrate the holidays, sharing the traditions which Mom established for all to enjoy. It's during this special season that we need to come together to embrace the wonderful memories of Mom.

With Jesus, you will never be alone. What will you do with the rest of your life? Will you choose to move forward or will you wallow in the past? I choose Jesus, who continually reminds me never to linger in the past for in doing so I may miss the opportunities in my present and future. What about you? The Bible says in the book of Joshua, "Choose you this day whom you will serve." Is it time for you to move on?

Printed in the United States
by Baker & Taylor Publisher Services